Treasure House 1

A Caribbean Anthology

Compiled & edited by
Veronica Simon & Barbara Applin

Contents

Foreword for the young readers

Here is a treasure house of stories and poems for you to enjoy. One of the most exciting things to do in a treasure house is to stand at the door and look around. What do you see? 'Wonderful things!' All different colours, shapes, sizes for you to choose and look at closely.

So stand for a moment at this door and look at the titles in the Contents list. Which 'grab' you first? Which do you think your friends will enjoy most? Or your brothers or sisters? Or your parents?

Then flick through the book and see if you change your mind. The titles gave you some idea of what to expect in a story or poem; perhaps the illustrations will tell you something different.

If you are reading this anthology at school, no doubt your teacher will organise the reading, and some questions in class. If you are reading this book at home, you will be able to go at your own speed, and you can decide for yourself what to read first. Before each story or poem there is a 'flash' with a question for you, or something to think about, first. At the end there are more questions to

answer, things to discuss or do with your friends or classmates. We hope that you will find them interesting and fun-filled. And – this may sound a weird idea – why not let your parents have a look at the book and see if they have any good comments?

You will see that these stories and poems vary a lot. They cover many different times, places and ideas, and they are told in different ways. Have you ever wondered about the people who write such stories and poems? Well, now you can find out in **Meet the authors**.

We suggest that you keep a journal in which you can write your thoughts about the stories, poems and the questions. Then you can use it when you read other books too.

And don't forget the **Afterword**!

Foreword for teachers

We are delighted to present you with a truly varied collection of Caribbean stories and poems that young readers can enjoy on their own or in a reading lesson under your guidance. Each is preceded by a 'flash' containing a pre-reading question, activity or discussion point that stimulates the appropriate schema and prepares the reader to deal with the ideas that are presented in the piece to come. Each is followed by questions and activities to stimulate higher level comprehension skills. These are also designed to give the young readers an appreciation of the way different stories and poems are constructed, and of how particular words are carefully chosen and sentences built up to create specific effects.

Apart from being the baseline for comprehension and vocabulary instruction, the stories and poems can also be used to teach any language concept and you will no doubt be able to think of many ways in which some of these stories can link to information and ideas in other curriculum subjects. For example, **Sense and senses** and **Catching butterflies** can introduce general science lessons on parts of the body, and the way eyes, nose or ears work, or on butterflies and moths; **Energy** can introduce a PE lesson; **Monkey business** can be related to maths lessons; **The zoo** can be used for a comparison between the life of an animal in the zoo and in the wild. Stories like **Tamboo bamboo** and **Wizz, Wow and Wuff** can also lead to practical activities like playing musical instruments or making carnival designs.

We often invite the readers to work out answers, or discuss points, with their friends or in a class group, and sometimes it can be very effective to ask everyone in a group to say whatever occurs to them on a particular point, write them all up on a board and then, perhaps, decide priorities.

The **Meet the authors!** section gives a chance to read some non-fiction material and to relate stories and poems to real people from a variety of backgrounds and with a variety of interests.

Readers could be encouraged to look out for more material by these authors and to write to them (care of the publisher) about the stories or poems they like or dislike, or how they feel about them.

Finally, when the book is finished, we hope the readers will go on to the **Afterword** and think over what they have read. Have their first ideas changed? Can they see any links between certain stories or poems, or make any contrasts?

And, if a class wants to send us a 'class report' of their experiences with this book, we will be delighted to receive it.

Foreword for parents

We hope that you too will be interested to look through this book and perhaps (if your children will let it out of their hands long enough) read some of the stories and poems. If they are reading this at home and not as part of a school activity, we suggest you leave your children the freedom to decide what to read in what order. They may want to ask you occasionally to explain the meaning of an unfamiliar word, to discuss some of the questions and to help out with activities. It is a good idea to read the stories along with your children and discuss the characters and plot. Some of them may remind you of other stories that you know or of events in your own life and you can talk about these with your children.

We hope that you will enjoy it too.

Sense and senses

Suzanne Francis-Brown

Close your eyes and think of how you would learn about things around you if you could not see. Discuss this with your friends.

I have five senses good and true.
Through them I know just what to do:
my eyes see all there is around,
my ears hear every single sound,
my tongue can taste drink or food,
my nose can smell things bad or good,
my skin and nerves feel all I touch.
Through these five senses I learn so much.

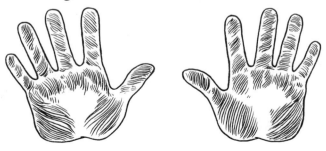

1

1 Which parts of the body are related to the five senses?

2 Write down the five senses. For each one, make a list of some of the things it helps you to find out about.

3 Do you know which animals have a very good sense of smell? Find out how that sense is useful to these animals.

4 Read the poem aloud. Did you notice which words sound alike or rhyme? Which of the rhyming words are spelt alike? Which ones are spelt differently? Can you find other pairs of words that sound alike but are spelt differently?

5 Try to write a poem like this about other parts of your body and what they help you to do.

Monkey business – a cautionary tale

Janaki Sastry

> Look at the first sentence. What would you warn your friends about, or what lesson would you want them to learn? Make a list with your friends or classmates.

Three little monkeys

A cautionary tale gives a warning or teaches a lesson – just see what happened to Chinni, Munni and Kunni!

Chinni and Munni were boys and Kunni was their little sister. They lived with their parents in a huge forest. These three little monkeys were healthy and good-looking. Their parents were very proud of them, and everybody who saw them loved them. They soon learnt to climb trees, jump from branch to branch, hang upside down by their tails, and do all other 'monkey tricks' that little monkeys do.

When they were five, the little monkeys were sent to school. They groomed themselves, threw their satchels over their shoulders, and happily trotted along to school. The first day was exciting. But soon the troubles began.

They just wouldn't get out of bed and get ready for school. When they finally did get up, one or the other had some ailment. One day Chinni would have a tummy-ache. Another day Munni would have a headache. Then it would be Kunni's turn, she would have aches all over her body.

Mum and Dad were worried and they took them to the doctor, but that didn't help. The three little monkeys missed a lot of schooling. Their friends could read and write and do all sorts of interesting things at school. But the three monkeys just enjoyed playing all day, and were not bothered about school.

One day Mum and Dad had to go away for the day. Mum left some food and six bananas as a treat for the three little monkeys and told them to play in the big tree until she returned.

The three little monkeys played a lot of games and enjoyed jumping from tree to tree and chasing each other. By midday, they got hungry, so first they ate their food, then little Chinni fetched the bananas. Now, as you know, Mum had left six bananas for them, so that they could have two each.

The banana puzzle

Although the three monkeys loved each other, when it came to sharing bananas – well, they were simply greedy. They began to quarrel.

'I'm the eldest, so I should have more bananas,' said Chinni.

'I'm the youngest, and I need more bananas to grow big and strong,' said Kunni.

'Bananas are my favourite, so I should have more,' said Munni.

Chinni and Munni pushed and pulled at each other, and began to fight. Kunni got scared and began to cry loudly. Suddenly, she heard a strange voice: 'Don't cry Kunni, I can help you all.'

The boys stopped fighting and looked around.

There stood a complete stranger – and he looked very strange. He was a huge monkey like a giant. He wore a long cloak and a red turban with a peacock feather in it. He had a very long tail, which he twisted in a coil and sat on.

The little monkeys were frightened. They just stared at the stranger.

'Don't be afraid,' he said, with a big smile on his face. 'My name is Jimmu, I'm Jimmu the Genius. I can solve any problems. I have come to help you.'

'Yes?' said Chinni.

'Well, go and fetch me the bananas.'

Quickly Munni gave the bananas to the stranger, and they sat quietly in front of him.

First of all Jimmu took off his turban and put it on Kunni's head.

'It's heavy,' thought Kunni, but she did not even blink.

Then Jimmu winked at the two boys. 'Here are fifteen bananas for us to share. Do you know how many we should each get?'

The three monkeys were puzzled. They tried to work out the sum on their little fingers.

'Three,' said Munni

Kunni shyly showed her three fingers.

'Then three bananas will be left over,' said Chinni proudly.

'That's very clever of you,' said Jimmu. 'I shall first of all get rid of the extra bananas.' In a flash he gobbled up three bananas. The children were puzzled and confused. Kunni tried not to cry, but tears rolled down her cheeks.

'But only three bananas are left, sir,' mumbled Chinni and Munni.

Once again Jimmu smiled. 'That's right. Now,

tell me how many bananas should each of us get?'

'Three,' they said together.

'You are so clever. These three are my share and I will eat them first.' He gobbled them before they could blink.

The monkeys began to weep, they were afraid to cry loudly.

'Right, I must go now. Call me again if you have any more problems to solve. Goodbye, my dear children. See you again.' Jimmu vanished into the thick forest.

When Mum and Dad returned, the little monkeys told them all about the stranger, and how he ate up all their bananas.

'Fetch the stranger!'

Mum and Dad went to complain to their King Sher. At once he sent his men to fetch the stranger. He was brought to the court. He stood there boldly and looked at everyone, grinning.

'Your Majesty, this stranger has deprived my children of their food. He has cheated them. He also trespassed into our tree when we were out,' said Kunni's father politely.

'That's not all, Your Majesty, he's also a liar. I left only six bananas for my children. This stranger told them there were fifteen and cheated them, then ate up all the bananas by himself. My poor children had none at all,' added Munni's mother, amidst tears.

All the animals and the birds that gathered there pointed to the stranger and cried, 'LIAR! LIAR!'

King Sher put his finger on his lips, asking them to be quiet. He thought for a while and then asked the stranger to speak up or face severe punishment.

The stranger came forward. He took off his turban and placed it on the floor and saluted the king.

'Your Majesty, my name is Jimmu. Jimmu the Genius. I come from a faraway forest.'

'Did you eat these little monkeys' bananas or not?' asked the Owl, the Chief Minister, who stood next to the king.

'Yes, sir. That I did. They were tasty.' Jimmu rubbed his tummy.

'You cheated the little monkeys and you are also a liar, are you not?' asked the Owl, twisting his spectacles on his nose.

'No, sir, I'm not a liar. I'm a juggler – a number juggler. That's how I made the six bananas into fifteen bananas. As for cheating, I didn't cheat them, sir. I took my share of the bananas and ate them, that's all, Your Majesty.'

'Well, sir! You call yourself a genius, then a juggler, even a number juggler. Show us what you mean or face the punishment,' said the king angrily.

A guard came forward with six bananas and gave them to the stranger. Jimmu put on his turban and knelt before the king.

'Number juggler! Number juggler!' whispered the children. They all came closer to see the juggling act.

Jimmu looked at everyone and smiled. He arranged the six bananas in the following order:

'Now, let's add them up. Who can help me? Is there a clever child who can add up?' asked Jimmu, looking at all the children.

'I can do any sum,' said Master Owl. His father was proud of him and pushed him forward. Master Owl quickly added up all the numbers and said, 'Fifteen.'

The king was amused. He burst out laughing. The three little monkeys laughed and jumped, others clapped and cheered.

'Well, sir! You are indeed clever. We do like your juggling act; you will not be punished for lying. But you will be punished for eating the little monkeys' bananas and trespassing.'

'Ah!' cried the crowd. They began to like the stranger, and they did not want him to come to any harm.

'Jimmu,' said the king, 'you call yourself a genius, don't you?'

Jimmu just nodded his head gently.

'We sentence you to teach our children in our forest school for three years. We order you to teach all your number tricks to all our children at our school,' declared King Sher with a smile.

'Hurray to our King Sher! Hurray to Jimmu the Genius!' cheered the crowd.

The next day, before dawn, the three little monkeys got up and got ready for school.

'I'm going to school, Mum. I want to be as clever as Jimmu the Genius,' said Munni.

'Me too,' said Chinni and Kunni together.

They ran all the way to their school. Mum and Dad were very happy to see them go to school again.

1 What warning would you give to the monkeys at the beginning of the story? What warning would you give to the stranger?

2 Do you think the three monkeys were really ill when they said they were? Do your little brothers or sisters ever pretend to be ill? Why? How do you know they are not?

3 Do you know any other tricks or games you can play with numbers? If not, ask your maths teacher or your parents or friends for ideas and play a number game with your friends.

4 How many bananas did the stranger eat? Did you expect him to eat them all? Why or why not?

5 Do you think Jimmu really was a genius? (If you don't know the meaning of this word, look it up in your dictionary.) Why or why not? Can you name anyone else who is or was a genius? Why?

6 Do you think the monkeys were different at the end of the story? If so, how had they changed? What lessons had they learnt?

7 Look at the list you made before you began reading this story. Choose something from the list and write your own story – either by yourself or with your friends or classmates.

Grandad's tickle-bone

Janaki Sastry

Have your parents or grandparents ever told you stories? What kinds of story were they? Tell your class group or friends what these stories were about.

'Tell us a story, Grandad,' said the children, sitting all around him.

'What story?'

'Any one,' they said. 'You tell nice stories.'

'What about a princess?'

'That's for girls,' said the boys.

'What about giants?'

'It's boring, all that thumpy thump, and grumpy grump,' said the girls.

'Then I have no stories left.'

'You do. Tell us about your hunting.'

'What hunting? Tigers or lions? Or . . .'

'Anything, Grandad. Please tell us a story,' begged the children.

'All right. Just one story,' said Grandad, twisting his bushy moustache with one hand. His other hand lay on his walking stick. 'Right . . .'

It was a dark, dark night. I was returning from the market. The wind was howling. The trees were

13

swaying from side to side. Ghosts were dancing to the howling wind.

The children moved closer to Grandad.

The forest was all quiet. The owls hooted at a distance. Lightning flashed over the forest. I was cold, and I was hungry. I was tired, and I had lost my way!

'Ah! What did you do, Grandad?'

I walked in the darkness. I ran here, and I ran there. I felt a snake slither over my feet.

'Ooh!'

'No, I wasn't afraid.'

Some way away I saw a beam of light. I walked towards it. The leaves rustled under my feet. The bushes tossed me to and fro. It was a frightening night. But I was not afraid. I walked towards the light.

The light began to grow brighter. I knew that I was near the house. I began to run. Run, run, run faster!

Suddenly, I fell in the river. The water was calm, and it was cold. I swam as fast as I could.

'Did you swim to the shore, Grandad?'

No, my children. I did not get there. A big crocodile swallowed me up. All in one gulp.

'Oh! No, Grandad! Did the crocodile eat you up?'

'Yes. Swallowed me up in one big gulp'.

There was a long silence. Slowly the children looked at each other.

'But, Grandad. You are not dead. You are here.'

'True. True, my children, very true.'

'How did you get away?'

'Did you kill the crocodile with a knife?'

'You hit it with your fists. Didn't you, Grandad?'

'No. No, my children. No.'

'How did you kill the crocodile, then?'

'I didn't kill him.'

'How did you get out, Grandad?'

'I'll tell you. Listen carefully.

It was all dark in the crocodile's tummy. I couldn't see anything. It was all slimy in the crocodile's tummy. I couldn't crawl out. Its tummy was rumbling like a lion's roar. The bones there began to rattle. The noise was dreadful. He was very hungry. I was very afraid. I began to think.

'What did you do? How did you . . .'

'Wait. I'll tell you.'

I felt around the tummy in the darkness. I began to sweat. Suddenly, I felt my big moustache and shook it with all my might. Then, the crocodile began to feel ticklish. He wriggled this way and he wriggled that way. 'Hee, hee,' he began to say between his teeth. He rolled over and over and began to dance, with a 'Hee' and a 'Ha'.

I shook my moustache again and again 'Hee, hee, hee' and 'Ha, ha, ha'. 'Hee, hee, hee' and 'Ha, ha, ha, ha'. I was tossed from side to side.

I held on to something hard in his tummy and it came away in my hand. It was a piece of bone.

Again and again I wriggled my moustache. Then I rubbed the piece of bone against his tummy. That worked even better. I tickled him without stopping.

He couldn't bear it any longer. 'Hmm, hmm,' he laughed, with his jaws tightly shut.

'Hee, ha, hum, hee,' he laughed between his teeth.

The poor crocodile could not laugh any more. He sure was tired of laughing between his teeth! He took a deep breath. Slowly his jaws opened wide. I could see the stars in the sky! All was calm for a minute. The crocodile held his breath, and I held on to mine.

Then, then, he sneezed with all his might. His jaws were wide open. Out I shot from his mouth, like a shooting star!

I fell on the bank of the river. I could see the lantern in my house. Your grandma was tossing it from side to side. I ran all the way home.

'Oh, Grandad, I'm so glad you're all right!'

'Then what happened, Grandad?'

Your grandma was waiting by the door. I gave her the piece of bone I had found in the crocodile's tummy.

'What's this?' asked your Grandma.

'Why, it's a tickle-bone,' I said.

'Then?'

I tickled your Grandma with the tickle-bone.

'Grandad, you are just making it up. Crocodiles don't sneeze like us, do they?'

'There's no tickle-bone, is there?'

'Yes, they do. And yes, there is. Do you want to see?'

'Yes, Grandad. Yes!'

'Right. You can see it. But you can't touch it.'

'Why, Grandad?'

'Because it's mine. It works only for me.'

All the children sat closer to Grandad. Slowly he unscrewed his walking stick.

Inside, it was hollow.

He looked at the children. Their eyes became wider.

Grandad slowly pulled out a thin bone from the walking stick. They all looked at it suspiciously.

'Is that it?'

'Does it really tickle?'

'Yes, of course.'

He put the tickle-bone back in the walking stick and screwed the top tight. He stood up and tickled each child with his walking stick.

They began to laugh, just as the crocodile had done. The night was filled with 'Hee, hee, hee!', and 'Ha, ha, ha!'

1 Why did some children not want stories about a princess or giants? What kind of story do you like? In a group, make a list of different kinds of story and find out which are most popular.

2 Why did the children move closer to Grandad? Do you think this was an exciting part of the story?

3 Grandad said he was not afraid. Do you think that was true? Why did he run?

4 The children thought of different ways Grandad might have escaped. Can you think of any others? Were you surprised by what he actually did?

5 Grandad described what it was like in the crocodile's tummy. Either act out being Grandad or draw a picture of Grandad there.

6 What was important about Grandad's moustache? What worked better than that?

7 What happened when the crocodile sneezed? Do you think crocodiles really do sneeze?

8 Do you think Grandad did make up the story? Give reasons for your answer.

9 Take turns telling your class group or friends stories that you have been told at home.

Why dogs chase their tails

Dwight Nimblett

> Talk to your class group or friends about your favourite animal. What kinds of thing would you do if you were that animal?

Next stop, San Fernando!

Rex, the dog, stared out of the train's window, as the 6.30 snaked its way uphill, then downhill – down towards the town.

'Next stop, San Fernando!' shouted the conductor.

Rex frowned, as he sniffed the mountain air. 'What kind of name is San Fernando, anyway? I bet this place is just as dull as the people who live there. But just wait till the Taylor family arrives! I bet they'll all want to make friends with us!'

Rex was wrong about the people in San Fernando. There, the residents were as colourful as evening rainbows. They were actors and artists, bakers and bankers, court clerks and cabbies, dancers and daredevils, too.

The best-known resident in this town was the rooster, Sterling, whose kindness was as legendary

as his beautiful tail. In his tail a child could see all
the colours of the rainbow. There were reds, greens,
pinks and purples, and every colour in this world.
Sterling was so adored by the townsfolk that there
were pictures of him everywhere. His tail appeared
on pet shop windows and village flags. His picture
could even be found on the sides of local buses.
Wherever the rooster went, the townsfolk would
greet him with adoring words and praise.

It was not uncommon to hear, 'Hey, Sterling,
thanks for planting the hedge. We were badly in
need of some shade!' or 'Thanks for the fresh-baked
goodies. I'll share them with my friends.'

'Don't you mention it,' crowed Sterling. 'Don't
you mention it at all.'

Almost everyone was pleased to have Sterling as
a guest, so it was not strange to find him nesting
restfully with Lulu, the owl, in the breadfruit tree.
At other times, he might decide that the abandoned
chapel was his home. The truth is, the rooster's
favourite perch was a rusted weather vane on top
of Ol' Jake's barn. Those who knew Jake could
understand why Sterling might take up residence
there, for old man Jake took in every imaginable
creature that ever wandered west of Noah's Ark.
There were pigeons and pigs, donkeys and deer,

cattle and catfish and puppies, too. And Sterling, of course, the talk of Ol' Jake's farm.

The only resident of San Fernando who wasn't happy with Sterling was Mrs Hodges, who lived across from the downtown square. Her lawn was never mowed, and her fence was stained and broken. Her entire house was boarded up, except for one window, from which she complained and spat and made such a racket that she hadn't had a visitor in years. Mrs Hodges was tired of all the attention that Sterling got, and she hated it!

'Oh, how I despise that wretched fowl!' she often thought. '"Sterling, you're so cute, and Sterling you're so smart",' she mocked. 'His picture here and his picture there. Ahhh! I'll pluck his feathers one by one. Just you wait and see.

The new arrivals

That day, the quiet of the morning was broken by the sounds of the first train arriving from Maintown. Puffs of smoke from her steaming engine greeted the morning air. It was summer, and children, there to meet relatives and friends, darted back and forth, sometimes too close to the tracks.

'Young man! You get away from there!' an excited mother shouted, as the train screeched to a stop. Stepping off the train was the Taylor family. The children watched as the town's newest residents made their way off the platform.

'One, two, three new people,' a little girl counted.

'Two people and a dog. Who are these folks, and where are the kids?' asked another.

Mrs Taylor wore a broad, friendly grin. 'Howdy. Good morning,' she called out.

Mr Taylor, a tall, lean man, clumsily juggled the family luggage in his arms. A few steps in front of them strode Rex, their pet dog, happy to be off the train at last.

'They're gonna love me – me and my bundle of toys,' Rex said to himself. 'I'm liking this', he thought, as he looked around. 'Just the kind of small town where I can rule the village roost.'

The Taylors soon settled into their new home. They spent the first day opening and unpacking boxes. On the second day, while Rex sunned his handsome coat, they dusted, swept, scrubbed and polished until their home looked shiny and new. For the next three days, Mr and Mrs Taylor carefully decorated Rex's room.

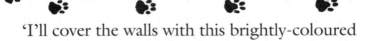

'I'll cover the walls with this brightly-coloured wallpaper,' said Mr Taylor.

'And I'll put the finishing touches on this quilt for his bed,' added Mrs Taylor. Then they opened his bundle of toys and laid them out around the room.

'Perfect, just perfect,' they both agreed.

But, even after all their hard work, Rex found that

nothing in his room was the right colour, the right size or in the right place.

'What ugly patchwork is this?' He pointed to the new quilt on his bed. 'And this fancy wallpaper makes my eyes hurt,' Rex said, as he looked around. Rex liked things his own way.

He spent several days rearranging his room. Then he declared, 'I'll soon be taking a stroll to that busy town square.'

The next day, before leaving, Rex stood before the mirror, admiring himself. 'I'm wearing my finest ribbons, I've packed my bag full of toys, and I've put on my golden collar. At last these folk will have the pleasure of meeting me,' he declared.

Rex strutted with his tail high in the air, sure that he would impress anyone he met.

As he strode past the fountain, he heard the sounds of laughter and happy children's voices. The noises were coming from a street procession, led by Sterling, the rooster. The children played their steel drums, and danced and sang. They were so taken with Sterling that they almost ran Rex over. His bag fell, spilling all his toys, but hardly anyone noticed – except, of course, Mrs Hodges, who was looking on from her half-opened window.

'Psst, psst,' she called. 'Hey you – you with the bag of toys!'

'Are you talking to me?' Rex asked.

'Couldn't help but notice how you were nearly run over by the rooster's gang. They're a bunch of troublemakers. Besides, as long as that feathered fowl flaps his wings around here, nobody'll ever know your name,' she warned him.

'What's it to you?' Rex asked.

'Just wondering why a handsome dog like you might be playing second fiddle to that fledgling of a bird. I mean, you're twice as nice and certainly much smarter.'

'You got that right,' Rex agreed.

'Come closer,' Mrs Hodges beckoned. 'I know the secret of the bird.'

By now it was story time and the children all gathered around Sterling, as they always did.

'What do you see?' Mrs Hodges asked Rex.

'Dumb children, who don't know how to read,' he declared.

'Look closer,' Mrs Hodges prodded.

'I see the stupid bird and those noisy steel drum thingies,' he said.

'Closer still, my friend,' she demanded.

'Oh! Feathers! I see the rooster's feathers!' Rex growled.

'You got it!' exclaimed Mrs Hodges. 'His beauty's in his tail. You get his tail, and you'll get his power.'

Rex has a plan

Later that night, Rex cooked up a stunning plan to steal the rooster's feathers.

'What a brilliant idea I've got,' he thought to himself. 'By the end of the next procession, those feathers will be mine!'

At the next procession, Rex hid behind a clump of bushes. Sterling sat as usual, with the adoring children all around. Rex could still hear Mrs Hodges' words, 'Get his tail, and you get his power.'

He lunged from behind the bushes and ripped the feathers from Sterling's tail. The rooster was taken by surprise!

'Ye-ouch! Ouchh! My tail! Who stole my tail?'

Oh what a commotion! The children screamed, as Rex made off with the feathers.

'I've got the tail; I've got the power!' Rex howled, as he disappeared into the bushes.

Rex ran and ran until he reached his home. He almost knocked over Mr Taylor, who was baking in the kitchen.

'These feathers are so beautiful and, best of all, they'll be mine,' he grinned, as he laid them on his bed. 'Finally, everyone will notice me. It is I, Rex the magnificent, who will make them adore me!'

Rex found some glue and, one by one, neatly stuck the feathers to his tail. There were pinks and blues, and greens and reds, and every colour in the world. Rex's room sparkled with colour.

Word quickly got around the village that the dog had stolen Sterling's tail. Several angry villagers gathered in the square, determined to bring the thief to justice.

'Don't you worry, Sterling!' declared a stout man. 'We'll get the crooked newcomer before long!'

'Curses upon curses!' shouted one strange-looking woman. 'In fact, curses upon curses to all dogs like him!' she continued as she began a witch-like dance.

Although Sterling was flattered by the villagers' concern, he did not wish any harm to come to the dog, so he quickly quieted the growing mob.

'Please! Please!' crowed Sterling. 'It's only a bunch of feathers, and feathers come and feathers go, but it's your friendship I'll cherish forever.'

After Sterling had pleaded for a while, the angry mob reluctantly agreed, then quietly dispersed – except for the strange-looking woman, who continued to cast her spell:

Curses upon curses to the dog with the tail!
Curses upon curses to dogs without fail.
Curses upon curses to all dogs, to be sure!
Cursed be their tails for evermore! she chanted.

After practising with the tail for several days, Rex was finally ready. He proudly paraded through the door – but, the moment he stepped into the street, there was an uproar of laughter.

'Ha, ha, ha – the dog with Sterling's tail!' some children shouted.

'Hee, hee, hee! What a strange-looking creature!' a woman giggled.

'I wonder if it crows?' the baker jeered. 'Cock-a-woof-a-doodledoo!'

Laughter was coming from everywhere.

Rex was humiliated. His brilliant plan had failed, and he felt even more alone. He ran, without stopping, until he reached the river. There Rex tried desperately to remove the feathers from his tail.

First, he wagged his tail as fast as he could, but that didn't work.

Then, he jumped into the shallow part of the river, hoping to loosen the feathers, but that was no use either.

In a frenzy, he tried instead to bite the feathers off his tail. Rex ran round and round in circles, but he could never reach that colourful tail.

Lulu, the owl, was nesting high in the breadfruit tree, and she saw the commotion.

'Who goes there? Sterling, my friend, is that you?' Lulu asked.

'No. It's only me,' replied Rex.

'Only who? Are you a bird or a dog? It's daylight, so my eyes play tricks on me.'

'Oh, it's a dog's life, all right, and it's just not fun any more. All I ever wanted was to have some friends,' Rex sobbed.

'Who am I to give advice?' asked Lulu. 'But it's really very simple. Before the handsome dog can *have* a friend, he first must learn to *be* a friend,' Lulu explained.

'I never looked at it that way. I thought my toys and things would get me all the friends I'd ever need. Guess I was wrong. But first I must say I'm sorry. If only I could remove these silly feathers!'

Rex chased and chased and chased his tail, but the feathers never fell off.

'No! Please, no!'

That same evening, Sterling, now without much of a tail, decided to take the long way home. As he strolled along the river bank, he almost bumped into Rex, who sat tired from the chase.

'Fancy finding you here!' said Sterling. 'Why did you steal my feathers? If you'd asked me kindly, I might have given some to you, in any case.'

'No! Please, no!' Rex exclaimed. 'I don't want these feathers any more! I only want to say I'm sorry, so sorry, Mr Rooster.'

'Oh, it's not that big a deal. It's just a bunch of feathers, and feathers may come and feathers may go, but it's friendship I cherish forever. Hey . . . join us at the next street party! I'll introduce you to my friends.' Sterling hesitated and then went on, 'Wait; we don't even know your name.'

'My name is Rex, and I'm the Taylors' pet.'

'And I'm Lulu!' interrupted the owl, high above.

'And I'm Sterling, the village joker.'

They all laughed together. 'Ha! Ha! Ha!'

'Hee! Hee! Hee!'

'Who! Who! Who!'

And as Rex laughed, one by one the feathers on his tail began to fall off.

'Yippee! Yippee!' Rex shouted, overcome with joy. 'I'm free!'

Rex and Sterling walked together until they

reached Main Street. Each step of the way, more townsfolk joined in. Then they held the biggest and happiest street party the sleepy town of San Fernando had ever seen.

And so it was that Sterling, the rooster, and Rex, the dog, became the best of friends.

Now, you too know for sure why dogs chase their tails

Curses upon curses to the dog with the tail!
Curses upon curses to dogs without fail!
Curses upon curses to all dogs, to be sure!
Cursed be their tails for ever more!

1 What did you first find unexpected about this story?

2 Imagine that you are decorating Rex's room and putting out his toys. What kind of wallpaper will you choose? Describe his toys.

3 Compare the characters of Rex and Sterling. Which do you prefer? Did either of them change during the story?

4 What musical instruments are mentioned in the story? Imagine you have come across these for the first time and describe them to your friends.

5 Why didn't Mrs Hodges like Sterling? Why did she tell Rex Sterling's secret?

6 Why did Sterling persuade the mob to be quiet when they were angry with Rex?

7 Do you think Lulu gave good advice? Why or why not? What lesson did Rex learn?

8 When Rex, Lulu and Sterling laughed, why did Lulu laugh, 'Who! Who! Who!'?

9 Do you think this is a good explanation of why dogs chase their tails?

10 Choose part of the story that would make a good illustration. Write a description of what you would like to see, or draw it yourself.

Energy

Suzanne Francis-Brown

Have you ever heard of energy? Talk to your friends
about some of the things we need energy for.

Swing your arms
round and round.
Clap your hands
without a sound.

Kick your legs
in and out.
Shake them
all about.

Bend your waist,
touch the ground.
Bounce your body
all around.

Lift your arms,
stretch up high,
see if you can
touch the sky.

Wring your face
in a frown.
Now smile wider
than a town.

Stretch your body,
twist and shout.
Let that energy
come out.

1 What are some of the things this poem asks you to do? Do you enjoy doing them? Why?

2 Take turns reading the poem in groups or pairs. While one reads, the other does the actions. How do you feel after you do the actions?

3 What do you notice about the lines of this poem? Why do you think they are written that way?

4 Why do you think this poem is called 'Energy'? Talk about where you have heard this word before.

5 Look for the rhyming words in this poem. Try to think of other words that have similar sounds. Read your lists to your friends or class group.

6 Try to make this poem into a song. Sing it as you do the actions.

Tamboo bamboo

𝄢 ♩ ♪ ♫ ♩ ♫ : ♪ ♩♪ ♪ ♪ ♪♪ ♫ ♪

Sherry North

> What can you use a bamboo for? With your friends,
> make up as long a list as you can.

What is it?

Leo tore the silver paper off his birthday present and
found a long, hollow tube of bamboo.

'Thanks, Pa George.' Leo stood the heavy tube
on one end. It almost reached his chin. 'What is it?'

Great-Grandpa George
wrapped his wrinkled hands
around the bamboo and
tapped one end on the
floor.

BOOM!

Leo gasped, then creased his forehead.

'It's my old bass bamboo,' Pa George explained. 'When I was about ten, like you, I played in one of Trinidad's best tamboo bamboo bands.'

Leo stared at the floor. 'What can I do with an old stick of bamboo?' he wondered.

Pa George saw the look on Leo's face. 'You're crazy about steel pan music, aren't you? Well, tamboo bamboo came first. We used to play alongside the brass bands during Carnival. If you can learn to play the bass bamboo, maybe you'll be a steel pan star one day.'

Leo shrugged.

'Would you be more interested if I told you this bamboo has a secret?' Pa George struck the tube against the floor two more times. BOOM, BOOM!

'What kind of secret?' Leo put his eye to the edge of the tube and looked inside.

'You won't find the secret like that! You'll have to learn to play and that means lots of practice.'

Leo took lessons from Pa George twice a week. He practised every day but, after almost a month, the sound was still not right. Each time the bamboo struck the floor, it made a sorry-sounding BUMP instead of a BOOM.

'The trick is in the angle,' Pa George told him. 'If your landing is sloppy, the bamboo will only grunt. You can't get a good sound unless you strike the floor just so.'

Leo pounded the bamboo against the floor again and again. BUMP, BUMP, B-BUMP. 'Will I ever play well enough to learn the secret?' he thought.

Leo keeps trying

One day, Leo took the bass bamboo to school. He found an empty classroom during lunch hour. 'If I can just hold the bamboo steady, maybe I can get the angle right.'

He hit the bamboo against the floor. B-BUMP.

'Sounds like a cat's hiccup to me.'

Leo looked up and saw Travis Sneed watching him. Travis was the kind of kid who would put a worm in your lunch or fill your school bag with sand, just to laugh at the look on your face.

Leo ignored him and banged the bamboo against the floor again. BUMP.

'Gee, what talent!' Travis said. 'Why don't you just give up?'

Leo walked towards the door, but Travis tripped him and grabbed the bamboo.

By the time Leo got up, Travis was out of sight. What had he done with the bass bamboo? Leo looked through the other classrooms. He checked under teachers' desks and behind bookshelves. He was about to look in the science lab, when Vicky tapped him on the shoulder.

'I think this is yours.' She handed him the bass bamboo. 'I found it in the girls' room.'

'Oh . . . Thanks, Vicky.'

'I didn't know you played tamboo bamboo.'

'I'm not very good.'

'Well, the bass is the hardest. I play the cutter – it's the soprano bamboo. My brothers play the fuller and the chandler. Maybe we should all play together some time.'

Leo shrugged. 'I don't know . . .'

'Just think about it.'

On the way home from school, Leo wondered if Travis was right. Maybe he should just quit.

Then he thought about the secret. 'Maybe if I play the bass bamboo well enough, my room will clean itself. Or, better yet, all the answers will magically appear whenever I do my homework. Or maybe last year's schoolbooks will turn into giant chocolate bars!' He decided not to quit just yet.

That afternoon, he had an idea. Maybe the key was not to try so hard. He wrapped his hands around the bass bamboo. Instead of slamming it into the ground, Leo held the tube as straight as possible and tapped the floor.

BOOM! The sound sprang out deep and clear. Leo jumped.

He tapped the floor again. BOOOOM!

Leo's dog echoed the sound. HWOOOO!

'Pa George, Pa George!' Leo ran to find his great-grandfather. 'Come listen!' He struck the bamboo against the floor once more. BOOM!

Pa George slapped Leo on the back. 'Nice work! I knew you had it in you.'

'Now will you tell me the secret?' Leo asked.

'Sorry, you'll have to figure that out yourself.'

Leo passed Vicky a note the next day.

Okay, let's give it a try.

Vicky passed the note back.

Come by my house after school.

Boom! Bang! Clap! Click!

Vicky's house was a few blocks away. Good thing – the bass bamboo was too heavy for a long walk.

'Do you practise every day?' Leo asked.

Vicky nodded. 'For at least an hour, before we do our homework.'

Two tall boys stood in the front yard, holding tubes of bamboo.

'These are my brothers, Patrick and Eric.'

Leo rested his bamboo on the ground. 'Hi.'

'Leo plays bass,' Vicky said.

Eric looked at Leo and nodded. 'That's what we've been missing. I play the fuller, this small tube here. And Patrick plays the chandler. It's bigger, but not as deep as the bass.'

'How many kinds of tamboo bamboo are there?' Leo asked.

'Fullers, cutters, chandlers and bass.' Patrick held up four fingers. 'The size of the bamboo determines the pitch. That's why the bass is the heaviest and the deepest.'

'Now that we have all the different sizes, we can be a real tamboo bamboo band.' Vicky picked up her cutter and held it across her shoulder. She used her other hand to hit the bamboo with a small wooden stick. CLICK!

Eric and Patrick struck their bamboo tubes with sticks as well. CLAP! BANG!

Eric looked at Leo again. 'Well, let's hear what you can do.'

Leo wiped his brow. He put both hands around the bass bamboo and tapped it on the ground. BOOM!

Vicky smiled. 'And you said you weren't any good. Let's try it together now, in order of pitch. You first, Leo.'

Leo tapped his bamboo on the ground, then the others struck theirs with sticks.

BOOM! BANG! CLAP! CLICK!

'Again!' Vicky yelled.

BOOM! BANG! CLAP! CLICK!

'Let's mix it up.' Patrick pointed to each of them in order. 'You, then you, then you twice, then me, then you again.'

BOOM! CLAP! CLICK-CLICK! BANG! BOOM!

BOOM! CLAP! CLICK-CLICK! BANG! BOOM!

Leo didn't notice when a dog across the street barked out the same rhythm.

After several weeks of practice, the new tamboo bamboo band played in the schoolyard during lunch.

BOOM! CLAP-CLAP! CLICK! BANG! CLAP-CLAP! CLICK! BOOM!

BOOM! CLAP-CLAP! CLICK! BANG! CLAP-CLAP! CLICK! BOOM!

Some of the students put down their sandwiches. Soon, all eyes were on the tamboo bamboo players.

Leo felt sweat roll down his cheeks, as he thumped the bass bamboo again and again. He kept the beat, while Vicky and her brothers jammed with CLAPS, CLICKS and BANGS.

After a few minutes, Leo noticed the tamboo bamboo beat was spreading. He looked around the schoolyard. Some students tapped their feet. Others banged spoons against cans of soda. A teacher tapped a pen against her notebook. Three cats miaowed and two dogs barked to the beat. Even Travis Sneed slapped his hand against his thigh.

That's when Leo knew the secret of the bass bamboo. Its rhythm was so right, every boy, girl, cat and dog within earshot had to join in. Leo had

turned the schoolyard into a concert hall and the
students into musicians, just by tapping out a beat
on his bass bamboo.

47

??? ♪♩♪♪♪♪♪♪♩♪

1 Write a description of a steel pan band. If you can, go to hear one and see if anyone will let you play a pan.

2 Can you play an instrument? If so, answer these questions. If not, ask your friends. What did it feel like when you first tried to play it? What kinds of sound did you make? How much did you have to practise?

3 Leo wondered what the secret might be. What did you think about his ideas? What did you think it would be? Were you right?

4 In the tamboo bamboo band, each instrument made just one sound. Look at the description of how they played together. With your friends, each make the sound of one instrument and try to follow the rhythm. Make up more 'tunes' of your own.

Girls do

Opal Palmer Adisa

Do you think girls and boys always do different things?
Talk to your friends about this. Try to think of things that
girls or boys could not do even if they tried.

I'm as pretty as a sunflower in the morning.
That's what Daddy says. He says, 'You're a prized
orchid.'

'No, I'm not, Daddy. I'm a bird of paradise,' I
say, standing very still.

Daddy is a horticulturist. It took me a long time
before I could say hor-ti-cul-turist. He loves plants
and flowers. He's the colour of his clay pots and
almost as tall as a coconut tree. Sometimes I help
Daddy garden.

He says, 'Alufa, girls shouldn't get their dresses
dirty!'

But my dress is already dirty and so are my
hands.

I'm a comedy with quick turns and funny lines.
That's what Mommy says. She says,
'Alufa, you're my favourite Alice Childress play.'

'I'm a poem,' I say, reciting Langston Hughes'
'I, Too Sing America'.

49

Mommy is an actress and she's prettier than rainbows and sunshine. She has long dreadlocks and she is the shape of an hourglass. Sometimes I help Mommy study lines, before I dash off to play.

'Alufa, slow down,' Mom hollers at me. 'Little girls shouldn't gallop like horses!'

But I'm off, running fast. I love to run, play marbles and bake mud cakes.

My hands, my knees, my dress, and even my hair, can get very dirty.

I'm a beautiful quilt with delicate stitches. That's what Grandma says. 'You my very special crochet spread,' Grandma smiles at me.

'Grandma, I'm that beautiful sweater you knitted for Grandpa,' I say, handing her some yarn.

Grandma Cathy sews and crochets. She has beautiful hands and the right side of her hair looks as if someone spilled powder in it. She has made me my favourite blanket. Grandma Cathy is teaching me to knit a scarf. When she looks out of the window and sees me on the tree, she points her finger at me. 'Alufa, little girls don't climb trees.'

But I am way up on a branch.

I'm a nine-handicapper. That's what my grandpa, Big Daddy, says. He says, 'Alufa, you're a perfect swing.'

'I am the ball sailing through the grass,' I say, watching Big Daddy take a swing.

Big Daddy plays golf with his friend, Mr Moore. He is tall like Daddy, except he has a moustache and he always wears a cap. Grandma reminds him to take it off when he is inside. Sometimes Big Daddy takes me along to play golf but I make up my own rules. Big Daddy fusses at me. 'Alufa, little girls don't go off by themselves.'

'I was on a special adventure, Big Daddy,' I say, as he takes hold of my hand.

I can't wait until we get home. I hang upside down on my best tree. My dress covers my face, but that's okay because I have shorts on. Next to galloping like a horse, playing marbles and baking mud cakes, I love swinging on trees.

I'm a one-girl siren who startles the entire neighbourhood. That's what Mrs Alston, our neighbour, says. She says, 'Alufa, you're my alarm clock.'

'I'm a drum in a jazz band,' that's what I think. 'Not an alarm clock.'

Mrs Alston is a retired school principal. Sometimes she makes me sit on her porch and read to her. She doesn't look like a teacher in her pedal pushers and sandals and fancy hairdo. She knows the right way to say all the words in my books.

'Alufa, girls don't scream,' Mrs Alston says.

But when Summer, my best friend, is coming over to play, and she is in too much of a hurry to look both ways before she crosses, I have to yell, 'Watch out, Summer! A car's coming!'

'Sometimes a girl has to scream,' I say to Mrs Alston as I run and hug Summer.

'Alufa, good thing you have a great big voice. I guess sometimes girls do need to yell.'

Mrs Alston watches out for all the children in the neighbourhood. She says we are all her students and the community is her school. 'I don't want to see either of you girls dashing across the street like alley cats again. Is that clear?'

'Yes, ma'am, Mrs Alston,' me and Summer say at the same time.

Me and Summer climb trees and ride our bikes.
I'm a leaf that blows everywhere. That's what Mr
Robinson says. He says me and Summer are bright
fall colours, and I think that is sure what we are,
orange and red leaves blowing everywhere.

Mr Robinson lives at the end of the block and
sweeps the entire street daily just because he wants
to. He says we need to keep our community clean.
'Little girls shouldn't pop wheelies!' he says.

Summer and me laugh and pop more wheelies.
We ride our bikes very fast, then brake suddenly.
Our wheels screech to a stop. Before Summer goes
home, I invite her to go fishing with me and Uncle
Ronald.

I'm an eel gliding through water. That's what
Uncle Ronald says. He says, 'Alufa, you're my lucky
charm that helps me catch fish.'

'Uncle Ronald, can't you see I'm a dolphin
gliding through the water?'

Uncle Ronald nods his head. He is a seaman.
He has a round belly Mommy calls a spare tyre
and he is always happy. Uncle Ronald has a boat
and sometimes he takes the entire family sailing.
He takes me fishing lots of times. 'Alufa, little girls
don't know how to put on baits,' he says, taking
my rod.

But I hold my rod and show Uncle Ronald
that little girls do know how to put a worm on

the hook. Me and Summer and Uncle Roland sit quietly and wait for the fish to bite. While I wait for the fish, I think to myself, 'Phew! Grown-ups sure seem to think there are lots of things little girls are NOT supposed to do.'

I'm an all-around girl who can do lots of things. That's what Aunt Carol says. She says, 'Alufa, I really like hanging out with you. You're my pal.'

Aunt Carol has an antique store and she repairs furniture. She mostly wears overalls and sneakers and she has a beauty spot in the middle of her chin. Sometimes I help her sand tables.

'Alufa, girls are good at everything, including fixing a chair, being pretty, making banana cake with coconut frosting, saying a whole poem by heart, being messy and having lots of fun,' she says.

And me and Aunt Carol have lots of fun fixing furniture, eating ice cream with her banana coconut frosting cake and playing all over her antique store.

But there's one thing I learnt little girls shouldn't do!

When I am walking Ragdoll, this boy named Michael keeps on following us and yelling, 'Ruff! Ruff!'

I tell him to stop, because Ragdoll doesn't like it, but he just keeps on. So I walk up to Michael

and punch him on the nose. That stops him, but he runs ahead and tells Daddy.

Daddy says, 'Alufa, sometimes you may have a good reason for doing something, but if it hurts someone else, it doesn't make it right.'

I have to sit in my room, all by myself, for almost the entire long, long, day just for bloodying Michael's nose. Ragdoll won't even keep me company.

As I sit in my room, I think about all the things that grown-ups say 'Girls don't do', and I wonder why. Girls are just like everyone else. 'Girls do lots of stuff,' I say out loud.

I'm a girl and I gallop like a horse, play marbles, bake mud cakes, get very dirty, swing upside down from trees, shout real loud, pop wheelies, dig for worms, go fishing, repair furniture and even sit all day in the room. So I stick my head out of the window and shout at the top of my voice, 'GIRLS DO! GIRLS DO! YES, GIRLS DO!'

1 Did you know what a horticulturist is? Did you manage to work it out from what Alufa says about her Daddy?

2 People describe Alufa in many different ways. Make a list of them and choose the one(s) you like best, to illustrate. Either do the drawing yourself or write instructions for an artist.

3 Make a list of the things people tell Alufa girls shouldn't do. Can you think of any other things people say like that? Do you agree?

4 What game is Big Daddy thinking of when he calls Alufa a 'nine-handicapper'? Do you think this is a compliment? Why or why not?

5 Look at all the things Aunt Carol says girls are good at. Can you think of any more? Are you good at all these? What about boys? Can they do these things too?

6 What is Ragdoll? How do you know?

7 Do you like Alufa? Would she be a good friend? Why or why not?

Bounce-about

Suzanne Francis-Brown

> Have you ever been to a fair or an amusement park? Talk to your class group or friends about the things you like best at a fair. How do they make you feel?

The bounce-about is my favourite place,
where I bound like an astronaut in space.
It's a cushion of air with walls around,
that guards me from danger of hitting the ground.
Inside it, I can run, jump and flip.
What does it matter if I should slip?
If I end up flat on the bounce-about's floor,
I'll sink in its softness, and bounce back for more.

1 What are some of the things you can do in a bounce-about?

2 Why doesn't the poet hit the ground when she jumps in the bounce-about?

3 Have you ever seen pictures of astronauts in space? Why does the poet feel like that in the bounce-about?

4 Write a poem about your favourite place at a fair.

All covered in soot

Yasmin John-Thorpe

With your friends, or in a class group, write an explanation of what soot is and how it is formed. If you don't know, look up the word in a dictionary and ask your science teacher to explain what happens.

Picking cashews

Lali Singh lived at the end of a short street in her village. There were three trees in the yard of her house: a mango, an avocado and a cashew tree. Her family owned the only cashew tree in the village. Lali liked all the fruits, but her favourite treat was roasted cashew nuts. Each year, Lali and her friends waited and watched for the small nut to appear at the end of each cashew fruit. The fruits hung from the branches, growing and ripening. When they were ready to eat, her father climbed a ladder and picked them.

60

On that day, Lali and her friends stood patiently below the tree, waiting to remove the nuts from the fruits. She taught her friends to twist each nut until it fell off the fruit. They threw all the nuts on the ground in the sunniest part of the dirt yard. The nut pile grew and grew as the children twisted off more nuts and tossed them onto the pile. After all the fruits had been picked, there was a mound of green cashew nuts.

'How long will it take, Lali?' her friend Shanti asked.

'My Dada says we have to wait for the sun to dry the green shell before he can roast them.'

'Yes, but do you know how long that will be?' Shanti persisted.

'No, I don't know. Let's ask him,' Lali said.

They hurried off to look for Lali's Dada. They found him stowing the tall ladder behind the house.

'Dada, how long will it be before we can eat the nuts from the cashew tree?' Lali asked.

'Well, if the sun stays hot and dries the shells, I think we could roast them in a week or two,' her father answered. 'But if we have rain, it may take longer.'

'Then we must hope for sun every day, right?' Lali said to her friends.

'Right,' they shouted.

'Why don't you go and eat some cashew fruit?' her Dada said to them.

'Yes, let's go and have some cashew chow,' Lali called. 'My Mammy makes it with lots of lime juice, salt and hot peppers.'

'Could you ask her not to add too much hot peppers?' Shanti begged. 'My lips burn if it is too hot.'

'Okay, let's go to the kitchen and watch my Mammy make the chow.' Lali took Shanti's hand and the group climbed the steps to the kitchen.

They gathered around the table as Lali's mother chopped the fruit into bite-size pieces and placed them in a large bowl. Lali passed a lime to her Mammy. She squeezed the lime juice and then added salt and a small slice of scotch pepper to the bowl.

'This pepper is very hot, so don't touch it,' her Mammy warned. 'It is just to add flavour to the chow.'

'Okay,' they chimed.

Lali collected a fork and the bowl of chow. The friends hurried outside and sat under the mango tree. They each took turns at stabbing a piece of the cashew fruit and popping it into their mouths.

'See, I told you my Mammy makes great chow,'

Lali stated, chewing a mouthful of the fruit. The others were too busy chewing to answer, so they nodded instead. Soon all the chow was gone. It was getting late, so the friends went off to their homes to dream of warm roasted cashew nuts.

Each evening they returned to check on the dryness of the nuts. Each day Lali's Dada shook his head. 'Not yet. Have patience.'

'Is it time?'

One week went by and then another. And still Lali's Dada shook his head. Finally, after one very hot day, as the friends walked into the yard, they saw Lali and her Dada poking pieces of wood into the pile of nuts.

'Is it time?' they shouted.

'It is time,' Lali answered, happily.

The group held hands and danced around the nuts. Laughing, they sang, 'Cashew, cashew. We're going to roast the cashew nuts!'

They made so much noise that Lali's Mammy and several of the neighbours came into the yard to see what all the fuss was about.

'You have to stand back,' Mr Singh warned the singers and dancers.

The friends stepped away and watched as Lali's Dada held a burning newspaper to the dried nuts and the pieces of wood. Soon a fire grew, until it engulfed all the nuts. It crackled and black smoke billowed into the evening sky. Lali and her friends backed away in fear. The heat from the fire touched their faces and the blaze lit up the darkening yard.

'There will be nothing left when the fire is over,' Shanti cried. 'It will all turn to ashes!'

'I don't remember there being this much fire before,' whispered Lali. 'And I was so looking forward to eating roasted cashew.'

'Me, too,' her friends said, sadly.

Just then, Lali's Dada moved around the burning pile with a long stick, poking at the fire. He used the stick to shift the roasting nuts from the top to the bottom. As he continued, the friends noticed that the nuts at the top had stopped burning and now they were only smoking. Soon the whole pile was smoking and the fire had died.

'Okay, get your crackers,' her Dada motioned to the group.

'You mean it's not all burnt?' Shanti asked. 'We can have roasted cashew?'

'Of course,' he replied. 'It is only the outer shell that has burnt off. Now you can crack the inner shell and find the roasted cashew nut inside.'

'Yippee!' the friends yelled, running off to find their favourite rocks.

Each returned and sat on the dirt near the smoking heap of nuts. Lali's Dada separated small amounts of nuts with his stick and pushed them towards Lali and each of her friends.

'Be careful, it will be a little hot,' he warned.

Slowly, so as not to burn her fingers, Lali reached for a blackened nut. The charred shell crumbled between her fingers, leaving another smaller unburnt shell. She used her small rock to hit the shell against the dirt. It parted and she saw a roasted cashew nut inside. Quickly, Lali popped the warm kernel in her mouth. Her teeth crunched the tasty nut and she swallowed. 'Great taste!'

All around, her friends were busy cracking and eating. Soon their fingers, hands, face and clothes were covered in soot from the charred outer shells.

The grown-ups laughed. Lali and her friends looked up to see what was so funny. Then they looked at each other and they laughed too. Lali could only see her friend Shanti's wide eyes and shiny white teeth. Shanti's face, her own face and her friends' faces were all covered in black soot.

1 With your friends or in a class group, make a list of as many trees as you can that bear fruit or nuts. Ask each person which fruit or nuts they like best, put a tick against the tree they name and then count up the ticks. Are you surprised at the result of this survey?

2 Why did it take so long before the nuts could be roasted? Do you know of anything else that has to be left to dry in the sun?

3 Write down the recipe for making cashew chow. Ask your mother what quantities to give for each item. With your friends or in a class group, each choose another recipe to find out about. Write them all down and discuss them.

4 Shanti thought the cashews were all burnt but she learnt that it was only the outside shell that was burnt. Have you ever made a discovery like that? What did you think was going to happen, and what did you find out?

Racing the rain

Joanne Gail Johnson

> Remember a time when it rained very hard and discuss it with your friends or a class group. Did you enjoy it? Why or why not? What did you do?

An early start

'Grandpa, look! The moon is following us!'

Sonny's grandfather glanced out the window and smiled. 'Well ay-ay, it sure looks so, doesn't it?'

'Unusual for the moon to be out this time a morning, eh?' Sonny's father added, his eyes carefully fixed on the busy, narrow, winding road.

'Why is the moon following us?' Sonny persisted.

'It just looks that way, Sonny,' Mr Beddow responded patiently. 'It isn't really.'

'I know, Dad, I know.' Sonny sulked a bit. He was restless. 'It takes two hours to drive from Port of Spain to Mayaro,' he thought. 'We've done this so many times. I'm bored with just listening to the radio and looking out of the window.'

Early on Saturday mornings, for as long as he could remember, his family packed up and drove to his uncle's cottage for the weekend. Sonny, his father and grandfather drove in one car and his mother, his sister and grandmother drove in the other. They couldn't all fit in one car since the children were growing older and there was a lot of gear to carry.

Dad's cell phone rang, 'Brrrring! Brrrring!'

'Let me get it! Lemme!' Sonny yelped.

Grandpa passed Sonny the phone.

'Yeeees! Sonny Beddow here! May I help you?' he performed his best telephone operator's voice. 'Steups. Wha you want, Tricia? It's fatty Patty!' he interrupted his conversation to update the others.

'Sonny, no playtime on the phone please,' said his father. 'And stop calling your sister names! Give your grandfather the phone.'

'Okay! Okay! I got it, Pa,' Sonny waved him off. 'Sorry, gyul, sorry. What? Oh, Ma wants to know if you remember packing the coal for barbecue or should we try to stop somewhere?'

'Uh-huh, I got the bag in all right,' said Grandpa.

'So y'all have binoculars, all right, nah!' Sonny bickered with his sister Patricia. 'So-doh, we have a radio and you don't! Na-na-na-na-na.'

'Sonny!' his father warned. Sonny clicked off and passed the phone back to his grandfather.

All fell silent again and Sonny thought he would go mad with boredom.

'Ay, look at the rain coming from across the hills up north east, Sonny. I bet we can race it all the

way to the beach.' Grandfather wanted to spice the
drive up a bit.

'Yeah, Pa, step on the gas. Let's race the rain!'

'This is as fast as we can go on these roads, son.'

'Oh gawsh, man. No fun!' Sonny complained
and then he began chanting out loud in a
monotonous voice, 'It's raining, it's pouring, the
old man is snoring, he went to bed and bumped his
head and couldn't get up in the morning . . .' On
and on he went and on and on they drove.

'Let's play *It!*', Sonny,' his father finally
suggested. '*It!* That's one mile post for me!'

'But Pa, you always say 'Let's play *It!* when you
see a mile post coming,' Sonny folded his arms and

71

sat back, not at all interested. 'It's not fair, man!'

'*It!*' Grandpa chimed. 'One for me too. Oy! Stop complaining and start counting mile posts, nah, boy!'

Sonny pouted, feeling left out, and joined in half-heartedly for some miles. Eventually he started singing again, 'It's raining, it's pouring . . .'

'Oh gawsh, if you must keep singing, change the track, nah!' complained his father.

'Okay. Rain, rain, go away, little Sonny wants to play. Sun, sun, come again. Shine on, shine out, race the rain!' Sonny laughed. 'I made up that bit.'

'Not bad, son,' his father chuckled.

'Ay, notice all those rain songs want the rain to go away, eh?' Grandpa pondered aloud. 'When I was small – and you too, Gregory,' he said to Sonny's father, 'we liked it to rain, eh? Man, we would play like mad in the rain.'

'Eeegad! Dat is cold and wet, man, gramps! You like that?'

'Well,' Grandpa laughed, 'maybe not now, but I don't remember caring much then. One time some school friends and I said we would enter this race some of the older college boys set up every year. It was cross country, all around Lopinot side. Well, it started to rain a nice set a rain, and that filled up the waterways just right. Next thing you know, we ended up swinging Tarzan style into the river we were supposed to cross as part of the race course. Dat was the end of dat race for us!'

Racing jockeys

'Ay, remember how we used to go race jockeys in the river there in St Ann's, Pa?' Sonny's father joined in enthusiastically.

Sonny was puzzled. 'Horses in the river, Dad?'

'Not horses, Sonny. Your dad made jockeys from palette sticks . . . er, what y'all call em now? Oh yes, "lolly sticks",' explained Grandpa.

'Lolly sticks? You raced lolly sticks? Y'all had no toys or what?'

'That's right, Sonny, lolly sticks! We shaved them into designs, maybe to have a bow and a stern, even. We painted designs and waxed them so they were waterproof. Then a whole gang of us from the neighbourhood would meet up after a nice rainfall . . .'

Grandpa interjected, 'Or better yet, if there was a nice drizzle!'

'Yup, and we would race them.'

'The lolly sticks?' Sonny repeated in disbelief.

'Tha's right! Ay-ay, you find that's . . .'

'Gawsh, kind a backward, man, Pa. And it's so dangerous down in those rivers. Y'all wasn't afraid you drowned or get washed away?'

'Well, of course, you're right, Sonny. Dis boy

watching too much a news. All them worries spoiling your fun imagination, child.'

'Now who's the killjoy, eh?' The two adults smiled at each other.

'In truth, Sonny,' his father continued, 'Ma and Pa warned us about going down to the river there in Carenage at certain times. There was one time I was standing on the bank watching the water rush down to the sea and the land by me slipped. It was scary. I could have been a gonner!'

'Well yes, two a y'all raced lolly sticks in the river!' said Sonny. 'Interesting . . . Oh-oh.'

'What's wrong, son?'

'Raindrops, Dad, raindrops . . .'

'Huh?'

'We're racing the rain, remember?'

The rain was close behind them now as they headed south on their final leg of the trip. All through Manzanilla, as far as the eye could see, the road was lined with coconut trees and between them the sea view played peek-a-boo. It was everyone's favourite part of the journey.

Up ahead, the ladies had stopped on the roadside and were passing round a pair of binoculars. Mr Beddow pulled over slowly and the three guys got out of their car, happy to stretch their legs.

'What are we looking at?' asked Grandpa.

'A savannah hawk, Gramps. She's beautiful,' smiled Patricia.

'Could be a he,' objected Sonny.

'Okay, Sonny, don't start now, you two,' Mrs Beddow hushed them.

'And what about *Mud Hog*?' Grandpa wondered aloud, as he peered through the binoculars.

Mud games

'*Mud Hog*?' the others asked in chorus.

'Dear, are you all right?' Granny teased, putting her hand on Grandpa's forehead as though to check his temperature.

'Sonny, you haven't had boy days until you play some *Mud Hog* or *Stick-in-the-mud* ... just soccer or catch,' Grandpa explained, 'but you play in the grass when it's soaked or, better yet, raining full force. It was more important to slide in the mud to tackle one another than to score goals! Oh yes, the good ole days!'

'Ooh, goosh, Ma used to be vexed when we came home!' Mr Beddow recalled.

'You sure right I was!' Granny laughed at the memory. 'I would hose those boys down under the garage shed before they could come inside. They had to scrub their own clothes too! You dirty them, you wash 'em. Not me an' that!'

'Eeyooo, it all sounds disgusting to me!' Patricia twisted her face.

'For once we actually agree!' said Sonny. 'Gimme the binoculars, nah! You had a turn already.'

As Sonny began to settle in and adjust the sights to focus on the hawk, the bird took off.

'Oh gawsh, man! That's not fair!'

'Follow it, son! Look! There she goes!'

'It could be a he!'

'Oh gosh, give me back my binoculars, yes,' Mrs Beddow was exasperated. 'The two of you will drive me batty!'

Seeing a sibling war brewing, Mr Beddow ushered them on their way. 'Come on, folks, let's make a move on! Come on, Sonny. Remember we have a little race game of our own going, eh? Maybe the hawk wants us to win.'

'Oh yeah! Sshh! Don't tell the girls! Let's go!'

They all clambered back into their cars and

continued their journey through the Manzanilla
estates towards Mayaro. The miles and miles of
coconut trees sped by and the thick dark clouds
billowed overhead.

'So, what's fun for you, Mister Sonny? Playing

some computer Gameboy with virtual rain and
digital mud?' Grandpa smiled at the thought.

'It's not as easy as you might think. I would
challenge you to a game, Grandpa, if you even
knew how!' Sonny defended his favourite pastime.

'Oh, ho, ho, ho, is that so now, young man!'
Grandpa winked at Sonny's dad. 'You can teach
your grandfather to suck eggs, eh? Well this is one
old dog willing to learn some new tricks. You're
on!'

'Come on, race the rain, Dad! Race the rain!' Sonny bounced up and down on the back seat.

Eventually the car turned off the main road and bumped along the lane, coming to a halt outside the simple cottage.

'Race the rain!'

Kerplop. Kerplop. The drops came down seemingly one by one at first.

'Weeell? What are we waiting for, boys?' Grandpa exclaimed.

As if reading each other's minds, all three jumped out of the car, tore off their T-shirts and made for the beach.

'Looks like a bucket-drop, Sonny boy! Ay, wait up, I'm an old man, yuh know.'

'I'm racing the rain, Papa Boy! Look, Dad, I'm racing the rain! Y'all on your own now! Fend for yourselves!' Sonny hollered as he sped towards the rolling waves. As the three splashed into the water, the rain clouds seemed to burst open and rain came pelting down.

The guys chased each other around the surf while the ladies, amused at their antics, stood on the porch and looked on.

'Boys will be boys, I guess,' laughed Mrs Beddow.

'Girls can play in the rain too, Ma.'

'Yes, of course we can, dear.'

'Ha ha – but who would want to?' chuckled Granny.

'Who won, Dad? Who won, Pa? 'Sonny called out as he splashed up and down.

'You know the fun thing about games like racing the rain, son?' Grandpa panted as he threw himself onto the sand for a rest. 'They never get old and everybody wins!'

1 Do you get bored on a long car journey? With your friends, or in a class group, list things you can do.

2 Why did the family use the phone? Can you think of occasions when you wished you had a phone? Why?

3 How did Sonny speak to his sister? Is this the way you speak to your brother or sister? What do your parents say?

4 How do you swing 'Tarzan style'? Is that difficult?

5 Look at the description of the 'jockeys' and design one of your own. Display all the 'jockeys' you can get together and choose the best.

6 Do you know any games like *Mud Hog* or racing the rain? What do you expect your parents to say if you play them?

Catching butterflies

Opal Palmer Adisa

Alufa finds a friend

When I was three years old, I told my parents I was going to be a moon man and float around the sky.

Daddy said, 'Alufa, you can't be a moon man, because you're a girl.'

'I can be a moon man if I want, and get blown up to the moon in a rocket and float around the sky like a paper plane,' I replied.

Mommy said, 'Alufa, you have to eat your beans and tomatoes if you want to be an astronaut.'

I told Mommy, 'I don't want to be an astronaut, and beans and tomatoes are yucky.'

That was a very long time ago. I'm seven now.

When I was four, Jamal moved in next door. He was four too. Every morning, even before I washed my face, he would holler for me. 'Alufa! Alufa! Let's go catch butterflies.'

So I told his mother, Mrs Moore, 'I'm gonna marry your Jamal and we gonna catch butterflies

and get blown up to the moon.' Mrs Moore looked at me like I was speaking a foreign language.

Jamal and I played all the time until I turned five. Then I got a brother and spent lots of time holding him and singing to him like Mommy did. Daddy said I was a good nanny. For a long time I was going to be a nanny when I grew up, but my brother started to crawl and didn't want me holding him all the time. Besides, Jamal was lonesome, so we went back to catching butterflies.

When I was six, our teacher read us this book about pioneers. So me and Jamal decided we were going to be pioneers, catch butterflies, get blown up to the moon and marry each other.

Me and Jamal wandered all over our neighbourhood, discovering new places to hide when we play hide-'n-seek.

Then Grandma Noelle, who lives in Haiti, came and spent three whole months with us. I had to pull Jamal to meet her. He acted real shy and giggled when Grandma Noelle said, 'Bonjour, jeune homme. That means "Hello, young man".'

Jamal shook Grandma's hand then and told her, 'Your hair is pretty, braided like that with beads.'

I begged Grandma Noelle to braid my hair just like hers. Jamal laughed every time Grandma Noelle said, 'Bonjour,' rather than 'Hello', and 'Merci,' rather than 'Thanks'. But Jamal and I soon started to speak just like Grandma Noelle.

One day, while Grandma Noelle was braiding my hair in cornrows with red and blue beads, Jamal said it was taking too long. So he went to meet the new boy who had moved next door to him. I told Grandma Noelle that Jamal and I were going to get blown up to the moon, catch butterflies, be pioneers and get married.

She said, 'Alufa, you should consider staying on earth, but Jamal is a fine young man for a husband. Pour ce qu'il a besoin c'est d'un chapeau de paille – all he needs is a straw hat.'

I went looking for Jamal after Grandma Noelle braided my hair, but he was so busy playing with the new boy, he didn't even tell me that he liked my hair. I stuck out my tongue and went inside.

Later, Jamal smelt Grandma Noelle's coconut bread and came by. Grandma Noelle used to be a baker so every day she baked bread and other goodies for me and Jamal. We ate bread with cheddar cheese and drank tall glasses of limeade, Grandma's favourite drink.

Grandma Noelle is almost as tall as Daddy. When she wears her straw hat, she looks like a palm tree, and her skin is brown like my crayon, but soft like my blanket. She taught me and Jamal to bake bread, so I told her we were going to be bakers, get blown up to the moon, catch butterflies and be pioneers. She said, 'You will have an exciting life.'

The new boy comes

Then that new boy started inviting Jamal to hang out with him to play baseball and he said, 'You can't play with us; you're a girl.'

Jamal didn't even tell that pear-shaped-head boy who had just moved next door to him that I was his best-best friend in the whole wide world and that I was the one who taught him how to catch butterflies. I was so mad at that Jamal that I threw the ball and hit him on his leg and ran home.

Grandma Noelle said, 'Jamal will come around, just give him time.' She offered to do my nails and played the albums of her favourite opera singers, Grace Bumbry, Simon Estes and Kathleen Battle. At first I didn't like that kind of singing, but after a while I felt the music filling my throat.

Jamal still hollered for me at my window, but most times he kept going. I looked out of the window as he and that new boy played baseball.

One day, Jamal didn't call for me, so I went to see if he wanted to play. His mother said he had gone to the park with that new boy. I was so mad with that Jamal I slammed his mama's door by accident.

I told Mommy, 'I'm not going to marry that Jamal any more. I can get blown up to the moon all by myself.'

Mommy said, 'You sure can, honey, but it might be fun going with Jamal.'

I got madder at Jamal when Mommy said that.

I went to Daddy and I told him, 'I'm not going to catch butterflies with Jamal any more. Besides, Jamal doesn't even know the difference between a tortoiseshell and mourning cloak butterfly.'

'Well, that your choice,' Daddy said. 'But you have been friends for a long time. I know he's hanging out with the new boy now, but you and Jamal have chased lots of butterflies.'

Daddy just didn't understand.

Just before Grandma Noelle left, she gave me a Leontyne Price CD as a present. I told her, 'I'm not going to be a pioneer with Jamal any more.'

Grandma Noelle cradled my head and patted my back. She said, 'Alufa, ma chère petite fille, my dear little girl, you should be patient with Jamal. Donne-lui du temps, give him time.'

I told her, 'I'm not even thinking about that Jamal because I'm going to be an opera singer when I grow up.'

I'm seven now and I'm taking piano lessons. Mommy tells me, 'Alufa, if you do real well with piano lessons, next year you can take voice too.'

Me and Jamal are still friends, but he mostly hangs out with boys and acts too cool.

Grandma Noelle has been back home six months now. She sent Jamal a postcard, but he couldn't read it because she wrote it in French. He asked me, 'What it says, Alufa?'

I just acted like I was deaf, but he kept on bugging me. 'Come on, Alufa.'

'Go have one of those boys you're always playing with read it to you,' I told him and I walked away.

But he followed me inside and Mommy said I had to read it to him.

Sometimes, when I'm walking by, Jamal calls to me, but I just keep walking.

Sometimes after I practise my piano lesson, I look out of the window and see Jamal playing with the other kids and I miss him.

A surprise for Alufa

But I'm going to have my picture on a CD just like Leontyne Price when I grow up and then that old Jamal will have to beg me for my autograph. That's what I was thinking one day, lying on my bed, when I heard some boy hollering my name. I looked out of the window and there was Jamal.

'Alufa! Girl, you best get on up and come on,' he called out to me. 'Don't you know we have lots of butterflies to catch? I spotted a painted lady and a red admiral.'

I didn't even answer him. Then Mommy came into my room and handed me a present. 'Alufa, this is from Jamal. He asked me to give it to you.'

'I don't want any present from him,' I said, folding my arms across my chest.

'Shouldn't you at least see what it is?' Mommy said, placing it on the bed beside me.

After she left my room, I picked up the present. I could tell it was a CD. I ripped off the paper and it was a CD of Denyce Graves, an opera singer. I hugged it to my chest. I guess Jamal is still my best friend after all.

'Jamal, I taught you everything you know about butterflies, I hope you know that,' I said, sticking my head out of the window.

'I know,' he said, grinning, hanging his head to one side.

'You think we will see a Gulf fritillary today?'

'I sure hope so, 'cause that's a really cool butterfly,' Jamal said, looking up at me.

'Jamal, I tell you what. If you listen to Denyce Graves' CD with me, later, I'll let you get blown up to the moon with me and we can be pioneers too,' I said, running to get my net.

1 What did Alufa want to be and do when she was three? And when she was four, and five, and six? Would you like to be and do any of these things? Why or why not?

2 What language do people speak in Haiti? Do you know any words in that language?

3 Look at Alufa's description of Grandma in her straw hat, and her skin. Describe someone you know.

4 What are tortoiseshell and mourning cloak? Find another one in the story. Do you know any others?

5 Why didn't Alufa want to translate Grandma Noelle's card for Jamal? Why did she do it in the end?

6 Do you think Alufa and Jamal ever did get blown up to the moon? Why or why not?

7 Compare the two stories about Alufa. *Girls do* is told in the present tense, while *Catching butterflies* is told in the past. Why do you think the author chose to do this?

8 Do you see anything different about the way Alufa behaves in the two stories? Does she act differently when she is with different people? Do you?

An island treasure

Yasmin John-Thorpe

> What kind of treasure might you find on an island?
> Discuss your ideas with your friends..

Morning chores

The island's lazy trade winds danced through the
trees. The rays of morning sunlight shifted across
the dirt yard. Bobo rested on his make-believe bed
of fallen coconut branches, playing a game of hide-
and-seek with the piercing sunlight that peeked
through the leaves. As the winds blew the leaves,
he closed his eyes against the glare. A warm breeze
tickled across his naked chest. He giggled.

'Robert Lewis? BOBO! Are you asleep?'

He jerked upright. He turned to his mother,
standing at the door of their home. She shook a
warning finger.

'Didn't you promise to have the yard swept before
lunch?'

'Yes, Ma,' he answered, scrambling to his bare
feet. He dragged the long branches behind the
house. He knew his mother watched his every move.
Bobo picked up the broom made from the veins of
coconut leaves. He began to sweep but he didn't feel

like working. He wanted to go down to the beach and explore the cave in the rocks.

In his misery, he swept fast and furious. Soon, clouds of dust surrounded him. Sweat ran down his face and naked chest. The dust stuck to him.

'You've done a good job today,' his mother's voice startled him. 'But you really got dirty.'

Bobo looked at the zigzag sweat pattern on his dust-covered body.

'Would you like to go down to the river and wash off?' his Ma asked.

Bobo nodded happily. He had only just learnt to swim and, even though he was afraid of the big waves in the sea, he loved to splash in the nearby shallow river, searching for small fish and tadpoles.

'Go on, but be careful of the incoming tide.'

Bobo's cave

Bobo raced off towards the river that ran into the blue waters of the Caribbean Sea. He wanted to wash off the dirt before he searched for tadpoles. As he splashed in the river, he checked the rock formation that curved between the river and the sea. There was an opening to a natural cave that you could only see at low tide. He told all his friends it was 'his cave'. That cave called his name.

'Bobo . . . Bobo!'

He often talked of finding treasure left behind by the pirates who once sailed the islands. But he couldn't explore 'his cave' before he had overcome his fear of the sea.

Bobo stared. His friend Alvin was climbing into *his* cave. Alvin had boasted about being unafraid of the sea. Bobo waited for Alvin to emerge. When he

didn't, Bobo got angry. Had his friend gone to find *his* treasure?

Bobo walked to the water's edge. He was afraid, but what if Alvin got his treasure? – he couldn't bear to think about it. Worst of all, what if Alvin was hurt and needed help? Bobo searched the beach, but he was alone. He waded in.

The waves pushed, then tugged, at his legs. Slowly, he inched deeper towards the cave. He dared not try to swim. When his feet could no longer touch the sandy bottom, his fingers clung to the slippery rocks. Finally, he could pull himself up to the cave's opening.

Bobo stumbled into the darkness, gasping for breath. He looked around the damp, chilly cave. With shaking knees, Bobo turned to the dark interior.

'Hel . . . lo?' His voice squeaked, echoing off the walls. He moved farther into the cave. He heard the waves crash against the rocks outside.

'Hello!' he called louder. It grew darker. Bobo's fear increased. His raspy breathing filled the cave and his heartbeats thumped in his ear.

'WHO'S THERE?'

Bobo screamed, pivoting toward the booming voice. He stared a long time into the darkness before he saw Alvin slumped against the wall.

'Alvin . . .?' Bobo questioned, leaning closer. 'Are you okay?'

'Oh, Bobo . . . I don't think so,' his friend answered. 'I bumped my head when I came in here. My leg hurts too.'

'Is it broken?' Bobo asked.

'I don't know, but I'm so glad to see you,' Alvin said. 'Did you come into the waves alone?'

'Yes, but I was scared,' Bobo answered. 'Why did you come into my cave?'

'I wanted to find the treasure for you,' Alvin cried. 'I didn't find any treasure and I don't think I can walk. Can you get help?'

'Yes,' Bobo answered.

'Please hurry,' Alvin begged. 'I'm sure the tide is coming in!'

Bobo goes for help

Bobo retraced his way down the dark passageway towards the light at the opening. He had to hurry. His feet sloshed in the seawater. The waves came rushing in and the chilly cave made his teeth chatter. He leant out. The sea had risen and it appeared too deep for him to get back safely. He could see no one on the beach.

A large wave rolled by the opening. It entered the cave and tugged at his feet. Bobo's fear grew. This was serious. If the cave filled with seawater, he and Alvin could drown.

His gaze searched the shoreline. A man came on the beach. Hanging out of the cave, Bobo shouted at the top of his lungs. The roar of the waves made too much noise and the person was walking in the opposite direction. Then the person turned and headed towards Bobo and the cave. As the man got closer, Bobo realised it was his father.

'Pa, Pa! Over here!' he yelled.

His father saw him. Quickly, he ran towards the sea. He dived into the waves and swam towards the cave. Bobo saw the waves roll over his father's strong body, threatening to toss him against the rocks. His Pa swam hard and reached the opening.

'Bobo, jump! I'll catch you. The tide is coming in and soon it will fill the cave!'

'Pa,' Bobo shouted, 'Alvin is in there!' He pointed into the darkness. 'He is hurt. You have to help him.'

'Is someone in the cave?' his father asked, unable to hear over the pounding waves.

Bobo nodded vigorously.

'Okay. First, I'll get you to shore. Then, I'll come back to help. Now, you have to move towards me. Ready?'

Bobo nodded and eased into the rough waters. His father guided his feet on the rocks and soon Bobo could cling to his father's shoulder.

'Get on my back and I will swim in with the next big wave,' his father told Bobo.

They glided through the wave at a mad pace. Water rushed up Bobo's nose and into his ears. He was flung onto the beach still hanging off his father's neck.

'Are you all right?'

'Yea . . . yes,' he answered, coughing. 'You have to help Alvin, Pa.'

'Okay, run and get your Ma,' his Pa begged, diving back into the swells.

Bobo got his Ma and they hurried back to the beach. They watched his Pa help Alvin out of the cave and into the raging waves.

Bobo hugged his friend when he reached the beach.

'You were very brave to enter the sea,' Alvin said. 'I'm glad you came into the cave and found me. If you hadn't, no one would have known I was trapped in there all by myself. Thanks, Bobo! But I'm sorry you didn't get your treasure.'

'It's okay. I found you, you're my treasure,' Bobo said to his friend.

I   How do you play hide-and-seek? Imagine that your friend has never played it, and explain what you do.

2   The broom was made from the veins of coconut leaves. With your friends, or in a class group, make a list of as many things as you can think of that can be made from the leaves, bark or small branches of trees. Make some and display them.

3   Think of a shallow river that flows into the sea. What kinds of creature might you find in it? Find out as much as you can about them and tell your friends or your class group. How different are they from creatures you might find in the sea?

4   Did you think that Alvin would find any treasure in the cave? Or Bobo? Were you right?

5   Did you find the story exciting? Have you ever been in danger? If so, tell what happened and how you were rescued. If not, make up a story yourself.

6   What do you think would happen after the story ended? Would Bobo learn to swim better?

7   Write instructions to tell a friend how to swim. Draw diagrams if that helps. (If you don't know, ask someone to explain it to you.)

Papa Bois' night school

Lee Kessell

Do you know anyone who goes to night school? What do they learn there? Would you prefer to go to school in the evening or during the night, instead of during the day? Why or why not?

The rain forest

Kizzy and Benjamin lived in a village on the edge of the rain forest. The village people grew all sorts of fruits and vegetables that they sent to the market in the town of Soufriere. The name of this town, as you probably know, refers to the sulphur fumes of a volcano, so it was only natural that Kizzy and Benjamin knew all about the spirits of volcanoes, as well as the dangerous beings who come to life after dark and prowl through the rain forest.

Do you think that the village children were frightened of playing in the rain forest, whether on a green-shadowed morning or a sun-filled afternoon? Those spooky creatures must be around somewhere! No! The village children, including Kizzy and her brother Benjamin, loved nothing better than running off into the forest, laughing and shouting and seeing who could reach the river first. They had a special place in the river where they all liked to jump and swim and splash and have a good time. All the children could swim like fish almost as soon as they could walk, so there was no danger of anyone drowning in the river pool. But at the first hint of day over, when the purple shadows reached through the trees like the arms of the long departed, the children were off, running, shrieking and screaming all the way back to the village. No one wanted to be left behind! So you see, the rain forest was a friendly, happy place during the day, but an evil, spirit world at night.

Kizzy was eight years old and her brother Benjamin was six. They went to the local school and Kizzy tried hard with her lessons. She liked reading and making up stories but numbers and sums made her little brown face screw up with concentration. Benjamin was just learning things like M for mat and S for sun and learning to count with matchsticks and his own fingers.

'Are the Douen for real?'

One day at school, Louise, a big, bossy girl in the sixth grade, came over to Kizzy and her friends at playtime. She began telling everyone, 'One night my mother saw the Douen playing in the river!'

'The Douen!' they shrieked. 'What were they like? Did they chase your mother? What happened?'

All the girls were talking at once and the teacher,

Miss Francis, came over to see what was wrong.

'The Douen!' she managed to make out. 'Louise's mother saw the Douen!'

'Oh Louise,' Miss Francis chided the big girl. 'You know quite well there are no such things!'

Louise gave her friends a knowing look. After Miss Francis had gone, she said, 'Oh, well, we all know quite well that Miss Francis HAD to say that the Douen weren't for real when everyone KNOWS that they are. The Douen, the mage noir, soucouyants, boloms, and all the other spirits, no one can deny that they come out at night and you'd better LOOK OUT!'

And that is how it all began. After supper that night, their mother put them to bed in their little wooden cottage (not forgetting to latch the window shut to keep out the jumbies that lived in the silk cotton tree at the end of the lane). Kizzy whispered to Benjamin, 'Benjy, there's only one way to find out if the Douen are really true or not, we will have to go and see for ourselves!'

Benjamin pulled the sheet up over his head and shouted, but not loud enough for his mother to hear, 'NOT ME!'

'Don't be such a baby! I want to see the Douen. What harm can they do? You know that they are children who died before they were baptised and they come and play in the rivers at night. They are just children like us.'

'No they're not!' Benjamin threw back the sheet and sat up and looked across in the dark to his sister. He could just make out the outline of her body in the bed. 'The Douen have their FEET TURNED BACKWARDS!'

'So what?' argued Kizzy. 'You think that makes them dangerous? They wear big straw hats and that doesn't sound bad to me!'

Both children were silent for a while and then Kizzy sat up in her bed and pushed the curtain aside. Bright moonlight flooded into the room.

'Look,' Kizzy said, 'It's as bright as day outside. We'll never have a better chance of seeing the Douen! We can easily find our way down to the river. Come on, I promise you'll be all right!'

'But what about those other spirits? What if we meet a coffin on the path? Or suppose we stumble across a toad with its mouth sewn shut?' Benjamin was shaking with fright at the thought.

'Oh Benjy, all those evil spirits only come out on DARK nights. This moon is as good as the sun for keeping all the jumbies and soucouyants locked up in their own homes. Anyway, I'm going, even if I have to go by myself.'

Benjamin was scared but he couldn't let his sister brave the night-time forest all by herself, so he gulped and shuddered a few times and just managed to choke out, 'All right. I suppose I'll have to go with you.'

'Good. Mummy's just gone to bed. I heard her locking up. We'll wait until we hear her snoring, then we'll open our window, climb out and run off!'

'I hope Mummy won't snore at all tonight,' thought Benjamin, but in next to no time he heard her bed creak and then soft and regular snores filled the little house. Kizzy got up, pulled on her shorts and T-shirt and very slowly started to unlatch the window. The metal fastening gave an awful squeak that made her stop dead in her tracks! The snores continued, so Kizzy, with a final yank, got the window open. Benjamin pulled on his shorts and T-shirt and was ready. 'They were going into the forest with bare feet?' you exclaim. That's right. Country children run about everywhere with bare feet and, if they get the odd thorn or cut, well that's just how it is.

Kizzy stepped out of the shadow of the wooden cottage and immediately felt the moonlight shining upon her like a spotlight! 'What if someone sees me?' she asked herself. 'I hadn't thought about that part of it!' She grabbed Benjamin's hand and ran with him down the path and into the shadows of the trees on the edge of the rain forest. The children's hearts thumped and their breaths came in great gasps. They waited to see if anyone had followed them. No. The cottages close by were all shut up tight for the night. The houses were quiet and still but, here on the edge of the forest, it seemed to Kizzy and Benjamin that the night had come alive with sound, and movement too!

Right above their heads was a krik-krak making the loudest cracks they had ever heard. Benjamin moved away from the trunk of the tree.

'I hate those things!' he said to Kizzy. 'They're so black and ugly and they have those awful spikes on their legs.'

'They can't hurt you, Benjy! They're just like big grasshoppers.' But Kizzy didn't like them either, so she took her brother's hand again and started off down the forest path.

Moonlight and night noises

Although the big full moon was high in the sky and throwing its clear white light all over the forest, the tall trees were acting just like umbrellas. The thick, dark green leaves were so close together that Kizzy's own mother could have stitched them into a quilt! Not much light got through, only where the odd tree had fallen down and taken a bit of the canopy with it. Here and there the path seemed to be blazing with light where a tree had been cut down to make the way easier. 'I didn't think it would be quite so dark and spooky!' thought Kizzy. She hurried from one blazing spot to another, and her little toes stubbed on roots and stones. As for poor Benjamin, he just screwed up his eyes and was dragged along by his sister.

Then there were the night noises! Apart from those nasty krik-kraks, there were all sorts of creaks and groans, snaps and rustles. A possum ran along a branch overhead with a funny squealing sound. Benjamin almost leapt out of his skin.

A big land crab clawed its way under the fallen leaves, making a scary sound like crisp paper being crunched. A nightjar squawked off in the distance somewhere. Crickets sawed their legs together as if playing fiddles and tree frogs sang along in harmony. The children never took any notice of the forest sounds during the day, but at night all by themselves, they heard every tiny scratch and hiss. The hair stood up on the back of Benjamin's neck.

'There's nothing to be afraid of,' Kizzy pretended to herself.

After what seemed like a long time, but in fact was only about ten or fifteen minutes, Kizzy heard the river running and falling in its bed as it

flowed from its beginning somewhere high in the mountains and struggled to find its way to the salty sea. It was a pretty, gentle sound and it made Kizzy breathe a sigh of relief. 'But now, what's that? Can I hear splashes and children's voices?' She slowed down and told Benjamin to be very quiet. 'I think I hear the Douen, Benjy! We'll creep up and see what's what. I want to see them before they see us.'

Kizzy and Benjamin crept along the path, their hearts thumping so loudly that they thought the Douen must be deaf not to hear them coming. At last the path opened out into a clear space and there was the river! But where were the Douen? No naked little children with their feet turned backwards and wearing large straw hats could be seen in the babbling river or splashing in the dark pool. Kizzy felt let down. Her mouth dipped at the corners and a big tear came into her eye.

'I so wanted to see the Douen!' she said.

Night school

Then, out of the forest rolled a deep voice like thunder far, far away. Kizzy stood up straight and looked towards a circle of trees where the moonlight fell into a clear grassy centre. Kizzy and Benjamin crept forward and, the closer they got, the better they could hear the deep voice. It sounded something like Sir's voice teaching the eighth grade history at school!

The children reached the first tree and peered around its large, rough trunk. There, in front of their very eyes, were the Douen! There must have been twenty of the little Douen, all seated on the grass with their straw hats keeping the bright moonlight out of their eyes, and they were listening very attentively to their teacher. But who was the teacher? Whoever it was had legs like a woolly ram standing up on its hind legs, all curly brown hair to his waist, and his top half was all muscle, just like the strong banana cutters who worked in the banana fields on the fringes of the town. He had little horns on his head and his voice rumbled out of his thick neck in a kindly way. He was telling his class something about the krik-kraks! Kizzy distinctly heard the name KRIK-KRAK!

Kizzy thought hard, then she bent down to Benjamin and whispered, 'It must be Papa Bois!'

Benjamin could only nod his head, his mouth open and his eyes wide, just like an owl's. All the country children knew about Papa Bois. He was the spirit of the forest. He looked after all the creatures of the forest and lived deep amongst the trees.

As the children's hearts stopped thumping, they could hear better and Kizzy became very interested in what Papa Bois was telling his students. He was explaining how the krik-krak was put together, what it ate, where it lived, how it grew up – well, everything! Kizzy crept around the tree trunk to

hear better and then Papa Bois looked right at her.

'And who do we have here?' He smiled across the grassy clearing.

Kizzy stood stock-still. 'No need to be afraid, little girl,' he went on. 'Come closer, I want to meet you.' And he held out his hand to her in a very friendly way.

Kizzy dropped her head down upon her chest and crept across the grass to stand in front of Papa Bois. Meanwhile, Benjamin had pulled back behind the tree and was shaking with fright.

'What are you doing in the forest in the middle of the night?' Papa Bois asked kindly. 'All little children should be at home in their beds, fast asleep.'

'I wanted to meet the Douen,' answered Kizzy in a whisper.

'Well, here they are! Say hello to the little girl, class.'

All the Douen looked at Kizzy, smiled, waved at her and shouted merrily, 'Hello, little girl!'

Kizzy looked at the Douen shyly and smiled, then she looked up at Papa Bois and said, 'I didn't know the Douen had to go to school!'

'Oh yes,' answered Papa Bois. 'I teach the little ones all they should know about the creatures and plants of the forest so that they never hurt or destroy them.'

'Oh, I thought the Douen were supposed to be naughty and we are taught to be afraid of them!' Kizzy looked at Papa Bois very seriously, with a frown on her moon-bathed face.

Papa Bois gave a deep rumbling laugh and all the Douen laughed with him. 'That's the trouble with the big people. They are afraid of what they don't understand. But come, little girl, and join in the class while I finish my lesson on the krik-krak.'

'My little brother is with me. Do you mind if he joins in too?' asked Kizzy.

'The more the merrier!'

And with that, Kizzy called loudly, 'Benjy! Come quick and join the class!'

Meeting Mr Krik-Krak

Benjamin's face peeped around the tree trunk, then his arm appeared, followed by the rest of his body. He ran quickly to his sister's side and they both took up an empty space on the edge of the group of giggling Douen. Papa Bois looked up into the tree behind his class and called out, 'Mr Krik-Krak, come down here and show yourself.'

There was a blur of black body and twirling wings and a large, grasshopper-like creature settled on Papa Bois' shoulder. He reached up, took it carefully in his hand and held it out to the class. 'Now, class, one by one, come out here and have a close look at Mr Krik-Krak. You may touch his back

113

very carefully and very gently. Be especially careful with insects' legs, because they break off easily.'

One by one the Douen walked forward and looked closely at the krik-krak and touched his smooth, hard back with a chubby, pink finger – just the lightest feather touch. After all the Douen had returned to their places, Papa Bois called to Kizzy and her brother,

'Come, children. Come and see your new friend, Mr Krik-Krak.'

Kizzy smiled at the creature and very carefully touched his dark back that was patterned like the rough bark of the forest trees. The krik-krak moved slightly, as if ready to spring away, but Papa Bois whispered to it, 'Everything is fine.' Now it was Benjamin's turn. He looked at the big grasshopper and he still didn't like what he saw. He hung back, his face screwed up.

'Mr Krik-Krak is waiting to greet you, Benjy. Look at his long feelers, they are nodding, telling you that he will be very disappointed if you don't touch him.' Papa Bois put out his hand, with the insect sitting calmly in his palm, and waited for Benjamin to decide – to touch or not to touch. Benjamin, who was a gentle boy, didn't want to hurt the ugly creature's feelings, so he bit his lip, put out a quivering finger and touched the armoured back. It felt as smooth and hard as his own fingernail, nothing nasty about it at all. He smiled and his eyes danced with moon stars.

'And now,' Papa Bois continued, 'I want you all to see how gorgeous the wings of the krik-krak are!' He gently pulled the tip of the wing and it opened out like a pane of thin glass, as orange-red as the heart of a flame, veined with delicate pencil lines like streams branching from a river.

Everyone sighed as the moonlight shone and wavered on the beautiful wing. Papa Bois released his hold, held his hand up above his head and the krik-krak leapt into the night sky 'He went so fast I couldn't see!' exclaimed Kizzy.

'And now, class, off you go and play in the river!' Papa Bois announced. 'But make sure you're all on time tomorrow because I'm asking my friend Miss Boa to be our special guest.'

The Douen clapped their hands with delight. It was a rare treat. 'Miss Boa can twist her body in all sorts of wonderful ways!' they said. 'Papa Bois lets her wind herself all around his body. And if we're good we'll be allowed to pat her beautiful bright scales and fondle her lovely head.' They ran off to play, laughing and shouting.

'Oh, Papa Bois, can Benjy and I come tomorrow too?' asked Kizzy with excitement.

'Of course! And bring along any of your little friends as well. I'm always happy to teach the children how to love my creatures and care for my plants.'

So Kizzy did just that. Next day at school (and, strangely, neither she nor Benjamin was at all tired after their night adventure) she told her best friends how she and Benjamin had met the Douen and Papa Bois and how Papa Bois had his own night school! Kizzy's friends couldn't wait to meet their friends of the forest and promised not to say a word to their parents or any adult about it.

'Grown-ups don't understand these things,' Kizzy told them 'and they'd be sure not to let us go!'

Everyone promised and they agreed to meet at midnight on the path just where it entered the rain forest. Well, Papa Bois' night school became so popular with the village children that he had to divide the class into two, with half attending one night and the other half the night after. And what about the dark of the moon, when only the stars spangled the black velvet sky? Papa Bois solved that problem by asking the fireflies to be ready at the edge of the rain forest to light the children's way for them.

To this very day, mothers and fathers who went to Papa Bois' night school now send their own children along. The rain forest is no longer a place of scary spirits at night, and down by the river the peals of laughter you hear are the mingled cries of joy of Douen and children having a good time together as they learn all about Papa Bois' forest.

1 Look at the explanation of the name Soufriere. Do you know the meaning of any other names of towns or villages or islands? Ask your parents, teachers and friends, and together make as long a list as you can.

2 Look at the description 'a green-shadowed morning or a sun-filled afternoon'. Why were the shadows green? Do you think this sounds better than 'a morning with green shadows or an afternoon filled with sun'? Make up other descriptions like this.

3 Do you think Kizzy was brave or foolish? Imagine you are Kizzy's mother and you see her as she takes Benjamin out into the forest at night. What will you say?

4 When Benjamin heard the krik-krak he said, 'I hate those things!' Do you feel the same way about any creatures? Why or why not? Did he change his mind when he touched it? Have you ever changed your mind? Choose a creature and describe what it looks like and what it feels like if you touch it.

5 Make a list of the sounds the children hear as they go through the forest. Why were these sounds so frightening? Imagine that you are somewhere at night – by the sea, on a lonely path through fields, in a

village street or anywhere else you choose, and
describe all the sounds you hear and how you feel.

6 What had Kizzy been taught about the Douen? What
do you think she had been taught about Papa Bois?
What did she discover now? Were you surprised? Why
or why not?

7 How would you describe this story? Frightening?
Funny? Sad? Real? Fantasy? You can use different
words for different parts of the story, if you like.

The zoo
Suzanne Francis-Brown

Do you know what kinds of animal are kept in zoos?
Talk to your class group or friends about your favourite
zoo animals.

In my mind there is a zoo
that I can visit any time.
And I'm going to tell you who
lives inside this zoo of mine.

There's a big, bold lion
whose coat of golden brown
reminds me of the towel Mummy used
to rub me down.
His mane is full, his roar is huge,
he's full of power and might.
They call him the king of the jungle
and I know they must be right.

Across the way, on an old tree stump,
the owls sit, still as wax.
Their round eyes stare suspiciously, then droop
as they relax.
They'll sleep a while, now that it's day,
they're not so fond of light.
But these sharp-eyed hunters
will be ready for the night.

120

The crocodile lies very still
near to the water's edge.
His eyes droop low, his jaws spread wide
as though propped with a wedge.
He seems related to a log,
but beware that sleepy face.
You'll rue the day if ever you
step into his space.

Behind a wall of glass and stone,
the snake lies languid on a tree.
Sometimes you really have to peer to see the snake,
so still is he.
The wonderfully patterned skin
hides muscles, now at ease,
But the sharp eyes and the flickering tongue
warn always – watch out, please!

The monkeys sit and contemplate
their visitors and what they bring.
If offerings aren't up to standard, then
away they swing.
They use their tails or hands with skill,
they gibber and gesture too.
But – careful how you mock the monk,
the monk may just mock you!

1 Is the poet describing a real zoo? How do you know?

2 Why do you think the lion's coat reminds the poet of a towel?

3 Do you think that the lion should be the 'king of the jungle'? Why? Are there any other animals that could be king? Discuss this with your friends.

4 What do you know about owls? Try to find out why they are hardly ever seen in the daytime.

5 What does the poet think the crocodile looks like? Why? Try to find more ways of describing a crocodile.

6 What do you think is the 'wall of glass and stone' where the snake is? Are any other animals kept that way? Why do you think it may be hard to see a snake on a tree?

7 What do you think visitors bring the monkeys? Can you find out what else monkeys eat?

8 Try to find as many pictures of zoo animals as you can. Write poems about some of your favourites.

Wizz, Wow and Wuff!

Jill Inyundo

What do you know about Carnival? Have you ever dressed up in costume, been part of a carnival band or watched the carnival bands go by? Talk to your class group or friends about your carnival experiences.

The bird of paradise

'Wow!' A voice, soft with wonder, seems to rise up from under the dusty old hedge. The hedge wasn't planted to make the garden beautiful. No! It was planted long ago by someone who wanted nothing to do with the people next door.

If you look more closely, there's the face of a boy peering shyly through the hedge. He has a smudge of grime across his forehead. The dirt makes his wide eyes bluer, his blond hair almost white.

'Wow!' he whispers again.

In the garden next door there is a lovely rosebush. But the small boy is not staring at that. There's also an old dustbin full of rubbish by the front door of the house – but, so what? A mountain bike is propped against the dustbin. But the boy is not looking at that either.

He is gazing at a magnificent bird that is

gliding down the front steps of the house, like a queen. Her blue and silver wings are held high. Her spreading peacock's tail is pink and yellow, studded with stars. Her head is flaming orange, with a curving beak, and it is crowned with a ring of shining silver feathers. On her feet are green slippers with pointed toes, each tipped with a tinkling bell.

In the garden the bird dances and twists and twirls round the rosebush until the boy's head is spinning.

Suddenly the hedge shakes and a little dog darts through it, covered in dust.

'Wuff! Wuff!' The dog pricks up his ears and lifts his tail high. His eyes are bright with curiosity.

The bird stops. She puts a firm brown hand on either side of her head – and lifts off the orange and silver mask.

Her laughing brown eyes look down at the dog. 'Wizard!' she exclaims. 'What's your name? Wuff?'

The hedge shakes even more and the little boy scrambles through into the garden. Now you can see that his hands and legs too are covered in London grime. The boy looks up and the girl looks down. They stare at each other as if nothing else in the world exists.

'Have you ever been to the Carnival? It's wizz!' The girl spins round and the bells on her toes tinkle her delight. 'This is my carnival dress! Mum made it!'

But she stops spinning and sighs. Lifting her peacock tail with great care, she sits down on the top step. 'Mum says we can't go to the Carnival today. My little brother has started the measles. So no one will see my dress!' She wipes a tear away.

The small boy is still staring. He puts out his hand and very gently touches the girl's curly black hair. With one forefinger he strokes her plump brown cheek. Satisfied, he sits on the bottom step and flicks a bell on her toe so that it tinkles merrily. Wuff licks the girl's other cheek.

'Well, you have seen it anyway,' she says. She strokes the dog. 'And so has Wuff.'

Then she scrambles to her feet and picks up the dog. 'I've got a smashing idea!' She opens the front door. 'Come on! I've got something for you!'

The boy jumps up and follows her, taking two steps at a time.

The girl leads him into the front room of the house. This is like the 'best room' in his grandma's house. But the boy doesn't look at the comfortable chairs, the thick curtains or the patterned cushions. 'Wow!' he says, looking down. Stretched out on the floor is a beautiful golden tiger's skin. He gets down and touches it carefully. It is made of crinkly cardboard.

'Put the tiger suit on,' the girl commands.

The boy throws off his jacket and gets into the tiger suit, zipping it tight. He turns to feel his floppy tail and then pulls the fierce mask over his head.

'That's wizz!' The girl laughs out loud as she opens her eyes. 'Just look at you!'

She turns the boy towards a mirror.

'Wow!' He smiles too.

'Look,' she points at each of them. 'Wow, Wizz and Wuff are all ready for the Carnival!'

The good-psalm-wish

'Shhh . . . we mustn't let Mum or Dad hear,' says the girl. The two children creep out of the front door.

'Let's go to my secret room in the cellar.' They go down the steps behind the dustbin. The cellar is dark and mysterious.

'Sit down while I light the candle.' The bird of paradise seems to shimmer as she sets down a flickering candle between her and the tiger. Wuff flops down, sniffing at the flame.

The girl whispers, 'You're new in this street, aren't you? Do you know about the Carnival?'

The tiger looks very fierce, but says nothing.

'Well, the Carnival is full of . . . it's full of people in all kinds of fancy dress. It's wizard! It's full of colour and dancing and singing . . . and laughing!' She makes a funny face. 'It comes from Trinidad. I was born here in London but my family comes from Trinidad.'

She leans forward. 'Now we must wish to be in the Carnival. Close your eyes!'

They close their eyes tight. Even Wuff's eyelids droop. In the secret room, the three no longer see the candle or each other. The cellar disappears.

'My Granny says that if you want something real bad you must think about it and nothing else while you say the "good psalm" over and over. So you

think of the Carnival while I say the psalm:
  'Give yourself to the Lord, Give yourself to the Lord!
  Trust in him and he will help you . . .'

The Carnival comes to life

Wuff tugs at Wow's hand. His bark says, 'Come on . . . let's go!'

The bird of paradise flies through the air, free. Holding on tight to her hand, the tiger follows. They leap through the concrete jungle from rock to rock, the little dog tearing along behind. The three friends race through the streets of London. They can already see, hear, smell and taste Carnival!

Up from the Underground stations come babies in buggies, old men and women, young couples and families, of all shapes and sizes and colours. People throng the pavements in thousands. Now Carnival floats pass along the roads one by one. Each is a moving stage, telling a different story.

'Ping, pong, ping, ping, ting, ping, pong . . .' the steel bands rejoice. Calypso choirs sing,

> *Forget all care*
> *and always wear*
> *a smile at Carnival time . . .*

And oh, the balloons! They float up, up into the air, calling the whole of London to this really wonderful Carnival!

There's no need to be hungry or thirsty. Wuff's nose twitches as the goat-meat-seller passes by. The bird of paradise is dipping her beak into a paper cup of fizz. The tiger's whiskers and paws are sticky with home-made coconut drops.

'Hey,' a voice cries. 'Just look at that paper tiger! He should go up front. He's our mascot!'

Another calls, 'What a wonderful bird of paradise! Hi! Come and dance with us!'

A little chap pipes up, 'And that dog! He's almost dancing!'

So the tiger leads the bird of paradise and her dancing friends. He twirls his tail to the reggae music while Wuff prances along beside him. The girl lifts her peacock tail for all to see and reggaes with her friends.

The lady-without-a-tongue

Meanwhile, behind the rosebush, the little house turns upside down.

'Rat-a-tat-tat, rat-a-tat-tat!' The knocking gets louder and louder. The house shivers in alarm.

'I'm coming! I'm coming!' calls Mum as she rushes to answer. 'Don't knock the house down!'

She opens the door. 'Well . . . Oh! Good morning!'

Instead of the bad-tempered postman Mum had expected, there stands the lady-without-a-tongue. That's what Mum calls her next-door neighbour, because she never speaks.

But she speaks now. 'My grandson?' The old lady is very upset. There are tears in her faded blue eyes.

'I don't understand,' says Mum.

'My grandson, young Sam! Where is he?'

'I'm afraid I have no idea, Grandma.' Mum doesn't even know the old lady's name.

'But I was told he came here.' The old lady hesitates. 'He had his little dog with him.'

'I ain't seen no boy or little dog,' says Mum.

'Sadie!' a deep voice rumbles from the depth of the house. 'The pot! The stove!'

'Oh, my goodness, the soup!' Mum opens the door wide. 'Come in! Come on in! I'll have to turn the soup down.'

The little old lady follows Mum anxiously to the kitchen. 'You see, my grandson came up from the country only yesterday. He's never been to London before.'

Mum turns down the soup on the stove as her husband comes into the kitchen. 'Your grandson's missing, Grandma?' he says. 'Maybe he's playing with our Gloria. Let's see.'

'Glory! Glory!' they open doors and call up the stairs.

Mum goes into the best room. No one! 'She must be showing off her bird of paradise dress. But where is she? And the tiger suit too?'

Grandma rushes past. 'Look! Sam's been here. There's his jacket!' She snatches it up.

'Now, Sam's Grandma,' says Glory's dad, 'please be at peace! If your Sam's with our Glory, he must be having a good time. And she's a sensible girl. She'll look after him – and his dog.'

Mum leads the way back to the kitchen. 'Come and join us in some nice hot soup.'

Glory's dad pulls a chair out for Grandma. 'Shall we say grace?'

Glory's mum closes her eyes. 'Give yourself to the Lord, my dear. Trust in him. Yes, trust in him and he will help you!'

The calypso band

Wow is getting tired of leading the bird of paradise and her swinging friends. He no longer twirls his tail round and round. It's hot inside the tiger mask.

'Hey, little tiger!' A tall young man leans over the back of the float in front. He shakes his mountain of dreadlocks in their neat ponytail.

The little boy runs up to the lorry. The large brown hand grasps the little tiger paw and pulls Wow into the float.

'What you need is a long drink,' laughs the man,

handing him a bottle of cola. Wow pulls off his mask and drinks the whole bottle thirstily.

'Now you can help me play!' The man gives the new drummer a drumstick.

'Wow!' cries the boy.

'Pong-boom!' The drummer taps his steel drum so that it answers him back with a deep bass.

'Ting!' Wow hits a smaller drum with his stick and laughs as it sings a high note.

'Pong-boom . . . ting, pong-boom . . . ting!'

'You've got rhythm, little tiger!'

Suddenly a bird of paradise flies up the steps of the float, followed by a yapping dog.

'That's wizard, Wow! Wuff and I thought we'd lost you!'

'Pong-boom . . . ting, pong-boom . . . ping-a-ling-a-ling.'

'Come on, little bird,' calls the man. 'Come and join our calypso. You two play the small drum and I'll play the tune on the tenor.'

When they hear the Carnival steel band
everyone gives a helpin' hand!
From those who're poor to those who think they're
grand!
Come, Wuff, and do your stuff,
come, Wow, and take your bow,
come, Wizz, lovely bird of paradise . . .

The goat-meat-man

Wow and Wizz are enjoying the steel band. How they love the rhythm of the music and the cheeky words the singers make up about everything they see around them!

But . . . suddenly Wuff sits up, licking his lips. Among the crowd, the goat-meat-man is carrying roasted chops on an iron skewer. Wuff throws himself off the float after the goat-meat-man.

'Wuff!' yells Wizz. 'Come back!' She grabs Wow by the hand. The two children jump down the steps after the dog.

'That pesky dog!' A clown on stilts nearly topples over as Wuff dashes between his feet in their giant-sized boots. Out of his hand flies a juicy goat chop. Wuff snatches up the prize and escapes as fast as his legs can carry him.

The little dog tears round the corner, followed by the children. And there is the goat-meat-man, sitting on a chair outside a cafe, with a drink in his hand. On his skewer only two chops are left.

Wuff sits under the goat-meat-man's chair, chewing his unexpected lunch.

The man smiles at the children and says, 'Take my last two chops. One for the bird of paradise and one for the tiger!'

'Wow!'

'That's wizzo!'

'Wuff!'

The meat soon disappears and the three are ready for more adventures.

Balloon magic

'Listen! 'There's a band in the park!' Wizz is holding Wuff in her arms. Wow is following behind, licking the sticky coconut sugar off his paws and humming the calypso.

'There's MC Brockie and DJ Det playing soca tunes!' calls the girl. 'Let's go!'

Families are picnicking on the grass. 'Come and eat with us!' they call. Children are playing can't-catch-me. 'Come and chase us!' they shout.

Det is on the mike. People are swaying to the sound. The bird of paradise twirls round, with a sleepy Wuff held in her arms.

'Wow!' The tiger sees a balloon-lady.

'Come and buy my lovely balloons!' she sings. 'Red ones, blue ones, green, yellow and purple balloo-oons!'

'Aren't they beautiful! Let's go and see.' The two children are too tired to run now. They walk slowly, hand in hand.

It's getting late and the balloon-lady wants to go home. So she gives the children all the balloons she has left.

As the balloon-lady lets go of the strings, the balloons rise. The three friends are as light as thistledown. Up into the air they go, over the river they float, and London town is spread out below them.

'Wuff, wuff!' 'Wooow!'

'That's wizard. Look! There's our rosebush, the dustbin by the door and Dad's mountain bike! There's home . . .'

Don't forget to give me the recipes

'This caraway seed cake is delicious, Sam's Grandma!' exclaims Glory's mum, enjoying one more mouthful of the freshly-baked cake Grandma has brought from next door.

'But nothing can be as tasty as your gunga soup and corn bread, Sadie!' says the old lady. 'Don't forget to give me the recipes.'

'One cup of cooked pigeon peas . . . two and a half cups of coconut milk . . .'

'Wuff, wuff!'

'What's that?'

'A little dog!' cries Mum.

The two women rush upstairs. But no one's there.

'Wuff, wuff, wuff!' The barking becomes louder.

The two women rush down to the best room. But it's empty.

'Wuff, wuff, wuff!' comes loud and strong through the best room floorboards.

'The cellar!'

In the cellar the candle flickers and flares, revealing two sleeping children and one wildly excited dog.

The tiger lies on his side. His hair is tousled, his tiger suit torn, his face covered in streaks of dirt and something sticky. The bird of paradise has crumpled wings and a bent beak. One brown toe pokes out of her shoe where a bell used to be.

'Supper time!' cries Mum. She gently pulls the girl to her feet while Sam's grandma picks up the boy.

'You must have been dreaming, Sam,' says Grandma.

'That's not Sam, that's Wow,' murmurs the weary bird of paradise.

'What a shame you couldn't go to the Carnival, Glory,' Mum sighs.

'That's Wizz,' corrects the tiger in his sleep.

But, I ask you, if the good-psalm-wish brought only a dream, then why the dirt, the broken beak, the torn suit, the utter weariness – and the happy smiles? Rather, the dream-come-true is that the lady-without-a-tongue found her tongue at last in the house behind the rosebush!

Certainly by now the dusty old hedge has been dug up. Forget-me-nots are planted there, with London pride in between. They were planted by Wizz and Wow . . . and are watered sometimes by Wuff!

1   What did you think this story would be about when you read the title? Are these good names for the three friends? Why or why not? What names would you have given them?

2   The story takes place in London, in England. Were you surprised that they have a Carnival there? Where did it come from? Would you enjoy it? List the different things that happen in this Carnival. What else could happen?

3   There are headings for different chapters. Are they good headings or can you think of better ones?

4   Why was the girl sad in the first chapter? What 'smashing idea' did she have? What does this tell you about the girl?

5   Why do you think the lady-without-a-tongue never spoke? Why did she begin to talk?

6   Do you think Glory's mum and dad were good neighbours or not? Why do you think that?

7   Find the part of the calypso that the steel band man sang about Wow, Wizz and Wuff. The wonderful thing about calypsos and rap is that the singers can make up lines about anything they like. Make up some lines about your friends.

8 Do you think there is magic in this story? Is the story exciting? Is there a difference between being magical and being exciting? Find examples in the story.

9 Sam's grandma asked for the recipes for gunga soup and corn bread. A recipe tells you what you need to cook something, and how you do it. Do you know a recipe for soup or corn bread? Write out a recipe for something you like.

10 Do you like the ending of the story, or not? Make up your own ending.

Meet the authors!

Suzanne Francis-Brown

I like to write poems and stories for children! I think that's because children don't mind if you take them into strange places, as long as you put in some rules so that things make sense. Poems written for children are fun because they're usually little stories with a rhythm and a rhyme. And, in some ways, they're like puzzles, where you have to get lots of bits to work together:

- So you have to work out what you want to say – the content.

- Then you have to figure out how to say it in a way that is special; a way that makes the reader **feel** what you're saying, and a way that connects to things they already understand.

- You have to work out a rhythm that fits.

- And then the rhyming words at the end of some sentences help to build the poem into verses or other kinds of sections.

Lots of the poems I've written came out of things I saw my own children doing. The first time I really paid attention to a bounce-about was when I watched one of my daughters, who could hardly walk, trying and trying to climb up and bounce. Sometimes, I was trying to work out how to explain something simply – like the five senses. Or I might just have been playing with words to see how I could catch a rhythm as well as an action. Then, of course, I've often visited the zoo. In Kingston, Jamaica there aren't many animals at the zoo, but children still enjoy their visits. I guess I wanted to try and capture some of the nitty-gritty: the lion's coat; the owl's stare; the way you hardly see the snake, even when it's right in front of you; the weird way the crocodile lies with its mouth wide open, for ages; the fact that the monkeys seems to laugh at people just as much as people laugh at them.

Think about something you feel strongly about, or something that attracts your attention, and write a poem of your own!

Hello! It's me! I was born and educated in India. My sister and I were the first girls in our family to go to school. We learnt anything that was available.

When we were children, my grandfather told us many stories about animals, birds and the stars above. As he told us stories, we could see all the characters of the story land in the fluffy clouds above. It was fun trying to find them hiding in the fluffy clouds.

Of all the stories, I love animal stories best – it's fun to see them behave just like us. I have seen elephants and tigers, snakes and snake charmers, monkeys and bears and many other animals and colourful birds where I lived as a child in India. Now I live in England with my family, a long way from India.

Some animals are clever, some are brave, some are cunning, and some are just simple, like a crocodile. Have you ever heard a story about a crocodile and a monkey?

Tickling is fun. Most children like being tickled, do you? I wondered if crocodiles felt ticklish too, then the story about **Grandad's tickle-bone** came to my mind.

Sometimes we are happy and sometimes we are sad. When I am sad, I try to do something different, like learning something new. That takes my mind off my sadness, and I feel happy again. There is plenty to learn; only if we try, we can learn a lot more than we already know. One day when I was upset about something, I sat

down and began to write stories. Until then I didn't know I could. Now I write in two languages: English and the Indian language called Telugu.

I make some of my stories into musical plays, and the children at our school help me to write songs and words for the play. We love working together, and then we do the play for our parents. Why don't you try to write songs and words for **Grandad's tickle-bone** and show the play to your parents?

I wrote **Monkey business** for James, a little friend of my daughter, to cheer him up when he was ill. My daughter Mahita and her friends John and James were three happy little children and were always up to some tricks, so I chose the three monkeys.

My main interest is mathematics and, quite often, to write a story, I first of all think of a number trick and then weave the story around it.

Perhaps one day I will come to see you all at your school. Would you like to meet me too?

Dwight Nimblett

I was born in Trinidad and grew up in the foothills of San Fernando Hill. When I was a youngster, San Fernando Hill seemed to rear up from San Fernando City and stretch endlessly upward. From my bedroom I could smell the rich brown earth that swirled past my windows and raced toward the clouds. This was my beanstalk. This was my backyard and playground. The youngest of three children, I was raised with my two sisters in the shadows of that hill. As girls, they tinkered with its mysteries, but that was never enough for me. So, left alone to do what any decent abandoned brother does, I imagined. I was Larry Gomes in the cricket season, and manager of Chelsea in the soccer season. I was Jacques Cousteau when the rains came, and a clay-footed Egyptian during the dust of the summer. And as I slid down the slopes of the hill in a blue abandoned suitcase, I'd made the Olympics at least three years in a row and I too tasted 'the agony of defeat'. Then, I was in charge of my own misadventures — the sole owner of my stories.

Now, in my day job, I work for Florida International University. I spend my days working closely with students — helping them to improve their study skills and to survive college. I am also chair of the Diversity Awareness Day Committee where we celebrate each other's achievements, communities and cultures. I spend most weekends on my Bayhen 21 sailboat, sailing up and down Biscayne Bay ... and wow, then 'I'm a kid all over again — misadventures a-plenty!' I enjoy the theatre, and performing on stage myself has had a big effect on how I feel about my creative work. I write plays and stories.

I write to escape from being a grown-up — searching for one last glorious misadventure and hoping that my two daughters, niece and nephew will leave their play stations and keyboards to dream with me. I am writing for them, to help them to understand that being a child involves weaknesses, jealousies, belongings and virtues. I write to invite them (and you) into backyard gardens to chase after butterflies, and bugs — and to discover **Why dogs chase their tails.**

Sherry North

On my tenth birthday, my mother's best friend gave me a flute. It took three whole months before I could get any sound out of the shiny silver tube. But once I made that first TLOOOOO, I couldn't put the flute down. Making my own music was so much fun!

Twenty years later, I also play piano and guitar. But my sense of rhythm has never been good enough to learn percussion, such as tamboo bamboo or steel pan. If you ask me what type of music I play, I'd have to say almost everything: reggae, pop, classical, rock. My stack of sheet music ranges from Bob Marley to the Beatles to Beethoven.

During a trip around the world, I had the chance to hear many different types of music: Polynesian, Vietnamese, Indian and South American. I found that no music puts me in a good mood faster than the music of the Caribbean. In my opinion, it is the happiest music on the planet. That is one reason I have travelled to more than a dozen Caribbean islands. From snorkelling in Tobago to climbing a volcano in St Kitts, I have always enjoyed ending the day with fresh seafood and live music.

I now live in Florida, where I write television scripts and children's books. Two of my books, **The School that Sank** and **Sailing Days**, are part of Macmillan Caribbean's **Hop Step Jump** series. I hope the story of Leo and his tamboo bamboo band will inspire some of you to find out how much fun it is to make your own music.

Opal Palmer Adisa

I was born in Jamaica and grew up there on a sugar estate. As a little girl I loved to wander off by myself. I was often called a tomboy because I enjoyed doing things that people thought boys did. I remember once, when I was about nine years old, trekking through the woods with a boy, hunting birds with our slingshots. We were gone all day, as we got lost. When I returned, the soles of my shoes were ruined and I had ripped my shirt and had scratches all over my legs. My mother scolded me. However, it was one of my best and happiest adventures. Another time, I went to the alligator pond with the boys and almost fell in out of a dare.

I wrote a story about that too, called, **Red Shoes and Alligator**. This story was published years ago in a journal in Australia and I wrote an essay about how I came to be a writer, called **Lying in the Tall Grasses Eating Cane.**

I wrote **Alufa** stories because I think adults often impose unnecessary restrictions on both boys as well as girls. However, I think girls have a harder time. I am working on more **Alufa** stories.

I have three children, and my youngest daughter, Teju, is very much like I was as a child, except more confident. There is nothing she believes she cannot do. I want to celebrate all the daring, non-conventional girls who dance with the breeze and use the sky as their measuring stick.

Writing is my life. I write stories and poems for children and for adults too. I have been teaching at college for many years and will soon focus all my attention on writing.

I love to ride my bike and walk. Those activities are very good for my writer's mind. I get ideas when I walk and work out characters. I live in Oakland, near Lake Merrit and it was while walking that the character Alufa came to me. I also love to dance, mostly reggae and dancehall, but salsa too.

Yasmin John-Thorpe

I was born on the island of Trinidad, one of nine children. I have six brothers and two sisters. From an early age, I loved to tell stories. At primary and secondary school, I would create a tale about kings, queens and princesses, in my head and keep my friends entertained with sword fights and dragon slayings.

I have travelled to and lived in many countries, first for my work as an airline stewardess on British West Indian Airways, and later as a wife and mother of two daughters. I've lived in cities such as Tel Aviv in Israel, Caracas in Venezuela, Far Rockaway and New York in America, as well as the Canadian provinces of Saskatchewan, Newfoundland, Ontario and British Columbia, where I now reside.

*I have been covered in soot like Lali and her friends in **All covered in soot**. I too have eaten cashew chow and have been frightened of the roaring fire started, by my dad, to roast the cashew nuts.*

*In **An island treasure** I gave Bobo some of my own fears. As a young girl, I too was afraid of the Caribbean Sea's strong currents on the northern coast of Trinidad. There is a rock formation with a small cave on one of those beaches, and I too wanted to explore the cave and find pirates' treasures.*

I am creating different stories for young readers, writing about my experiences in other countries, and hoping that readers everywhere will enjoy these adventures.

Joanne Gail Johnson

I was born and bred in Trinidad. My father grew up in Grenada. As a young man, he worked in Guyana, Barbados, Bahamas, and finally Trinidad, where he met my mother and has lived ever since. Together they have inspired me to respect my own feeling of belonging to the Caribbean. I have travelled to many of our islands, including Grenada, Barbados, St Vincent and the Grenadines, St Lucia, Antigua, Jamaica and the Cayman Islands and, of course, our sister isle, Tobago.

I began keeping journals when I was twelve and I still have notebooks and diaries from as far back as 1992. As a child, I preferred a quiet corner and a book and often came alive only to act out stories with props and costumes, trying out my scripts with imaginary characters. As a primary school teacher, I started the school newsletter, and became involved in Theatre in Education. I liked to get away from the traditional classroom setting through theatre, computers and electronic media. My dreams came true, when I wrote and produced The island, an interactive play for children about our national bird, the scarlet ibis, which is in danger from illegal hunters.

I have worked in advertising and written and produced scripts for television. I also write for the women's quarterly, She Caribbean magazine. Macmillan has published my

children's stories, Go Barefoot, The Scottish Island Girl, Sally's Way and Digger's Diner. The next story, adapted from my play, will be Ibis Stew? Oh, No!

My story in this anthology, Racing the rain, pretty much wrote itself, as they say. Since many of us spend so much time on the road, I wanted to write a story for young children that took place mostly as a conversation between travellers in a car. Since I recently had a son, I also wanted to write a story that honours and reflects healthy male relationships.

I remembered seventeen years ago driving my nephew Matthew to school every morning when he was just four years old. He used to look out of the window and entertain me with songs he would make up about what he saw. One day he noticed the moon was still out and asked me why it was following us. It was a delightful moment I have never forgotten and I allowed the memory to inspire me. As I began writing, I looked out of the window to see a light rain moving across the hills towards my house. I thought I heard his young voice sing, 'Let's race the rain, Aunty Jo!' and the title Racing the rain came to me. The story developed naturally and was completed within a couple of hours!

Lee Kessell

You can call me Lee, all my friends do. I once asked a young boy I was teaching what he liked best and he said, 'The smell of my computer booting up in the morning.' I wonder what you like? I like scuba diving better even than sailing. I just love anything to do with the sea, but being under it saying hello to all the fishes is great fun. I was born by the sea in Australia and learnt to swim before I could even walk. I've always been adventurous and so has my husband, and that is how we eventually came to live in the Caribbean.

At first we built a house deep in the forest in Trinidad and then we moved up to St Lucia and lived on a boat. Well, my pupils all thought I was mad and I wonder how you would like living on a boat? It can get rough and scary but most of the time I loved it. Our two young sons didn't like living on a boat, I can tell you, especially when we moved away from the dock and anchored out in the bay and they had to row to shore!

I think I wrote my first poem when I was five and I've been writing ever since. By the time I stopped teaching, I was lecturing to university students! But you know what? I like writing for children like you. In fact, that's what I like best of all.

Now, if you're curious about how I came to write **Papa Bois' night school**, it so happened that, while I was teaching in Trinidad, I came across a lovely painting by a local artist showing Papa Bois, the Douen, Madam D'Glow and other night-time creatures happily together in the green forest night. Remembering that picture, I suddenly thought what fun it would be to tell you all that Papa Bois and his friends are your friends and all that Papa Bois wants is to see his forest loved and cared for. How best to teach us humans the lessons of the forest? By teaching those frisky little Douen at night school, of course!

I come from the sun-drenched hills of the Western Rift Valley of East Africa, which rise above the north eastern shores of Lake Victoria in Kenya. This is where my husband, Weboko, was born and brought up. This is where we farm the land that will be inherited by our sons, Kwame and Boko, and our little grandson, Baxter Weboko. In Kenya I have taught students in secondary schools, in primary teacher training colleges, in secondary teacher training colleges and the university. I have counselled students since I arrived here in 1963, Independence Day! I have written and produced plays for drama festivals. I have written history books about our continent and I have written a string of stories about our people for children, teenagers and adults. I love writing about Africa.

But I was born and brought up in London. People call London 'the smoke' because it is a huge city, full of shops and factories, which trades with the world and is full of history . . . and dirt! I love London town and, because I am African as well as English, I always try to come back to London at Carnival time each August Bank Holiday. I thought about this story first when I

went to the Carnival with my friends from St Kitts. The next time, I went with my friends from Trinidad and they said, 'You must write about the colour, calypso and coconut drops of the Notting Hill Carnival, Jill!' And so, I found myself thinking about Wizz and Wow and Wuff and the good-wish-psalm that made the lady-without-a-tongue talk to her neighbours next door behind the rose bush!

I wrote this story for my friends from St Kitts and Trinidad, for my grandchildren in East Africa – Abigail, Faith, Vicky, Manu and Abum Inyangala – and for my little grandson, Baxter Weboko, who lives in London and will no doubt soon be swinging to the Carnival steel bands! But, above all, I wrote this story for all of you in the sun-soaked islands of the Caribbean, so you will know that your songs and dances, warmth and companionship brighten up the stone streets of London and bring healing between neighbours there!

Afterword

Before you leave this treasure house, take a moment to look back and reflect on what you have experienced. You may like to discuss the following questions with your friends or class group, and write up your thoughts in your journal.

- 📖 Which story or poem did you like the most? Which did you like the least? Why?

- 📖 Did any of the stories make you laugh? Why? Are you – or your friends – like any of the characters in these stories?

- 📖 Do you agree that some stories are for girls and some for boys? Count the number of girls and the number of boys in your class. Find out how many girls and how many boys enjoyed each story or poem in this anthology.

- 📖 Have your grandparents told any of you the same stories? If so, did you notice any differences in the way they were told?

- 📖 The story about Rex explains why dogs chase their tails. Can you make up a story of your own to explain something else that an animal does?

📖 Compare the way a dog is shown in **Why dogs chase their tails** and **Wizz, Wow and Wuff**. Which dog do you prefer? Why?

📖 There are two stories about the same girl. Have you read other sets of stories about one character? Would you like to read more about another character in this anthology? Imagine what the story might be about.

📖 **Wizz, Wow and Wuff** takes place in London. Have you read any other stories that do not take place in the Caribbean? What did you learn from them about other countries? Did anything surprise you?

📖 Look at the poems in this anthology. With your friends, or in your class, read them aloud. Which do you like best? Why? What is different about the rhythms and the length of the lines? Why do the poets use rhyme?

📖 Finally, make a note in your journal of what you have discovered about writing stories and poems, and start to work out some of your own.

Macmillan Education
Between Towns Road, Oxford OX4 3PP
A division of Macmillan Publishers Limited
Companies and representatives throughout the world

www.macmillan-caribbean.com

ISBN-13: 978-14050-309-46
ISBN-10: 1-4050-3094-1

Edited by Veronica Simon and Barbara Applin

Designed by Holbrook Design Oxford Ltd
Illustrated by Tim Stevens
Cover design by Bob Swan/Karen Hamer
Cover illustration by Tim Stevens

Printed and bound in Thailand

2010 2009 2008 2007 2006
10 9 8 7 6 5 4 3 2 1